THE EVERYDAY LIFE OF THE
AZTEC & MAYA

THE EVERYDAY LIFE OF THE
AZTEC & MAYA

An expert account of the great Central American civilizations with over 200 magnificent photographs and illustrations, and 30 maps, plans and drawings

AUTHOR: CHARLES PHILLIPS • CONSULTANT: DAVID M JONES

southwater

This edition is published by Southwater, an imprint of Anness Publishing Ltd, Hermes House, 88–89 Blackfriars Road, London SE1 8HA; tel. 020 7401 2077; fax 020 7633 9499

www.southwaterbooks.com; www.annesspublishing.com

Anness Publishing has a new picture agency outlet for images for publishing, promotions or advertising. Please visit our website www.practicalpictures.com for more information.

UK agent: The Manning Partnership Ltd; tel. 01225 478444; fax 01225 478440; sales@manning-partnership.co.uk
UK distributor: Grantham Book Services Ltd; tel. 01476 541080; fax 01476 541061; orders@gbs.tbs-ltd.co.uk
North American agent/distributor: National Book Network; tel. 301 459 3366; fax 301 429 5746; www.nbnbooks.com
Australian agent/distributor: Pan Macmillan Australia; tel. 1300 135 113; fax 1300 135 103; customer.service@macmillan.com.au
New Zealand agent/distributor: David Bateman Ltd; tel. (09) 415 7664; fax (09) 415 8892

Publisher: Joanna Lorenz
Senior Managing Editor: Conor Kilgallon
Editor: Joy Wotton
Designer: Nigel Partridge
Illustrators: Peter Bull Art Studios, Vanessa Card
Production Controller: Wendy Lawson

ETHICAL TRADING POLICY
At Anness Publishing we believe that business should be conducted in an ethical and ecologically sustainable way, with respect for the environment and a proper regard to the replacement of the natural resources we employ.
As a publisher, we use a lot of wood pulp to make high-quality paper for printing, and that wood commonly comes from spruce trees. We are therefore currently growing more than 500,000 trees in two Scottish forest plantations near Aberdeen – Berrymoss (130 hectares/320 acres) and West Touxhill (125 hectares/305 acres). The forests we manage contain twice the number of trees employed each year in paper-making for our books. Because of this ongoing ecological investment programme, you, as our customer, can have the pleasure and reassurance of knowing that a tree is being cultivated on your behalf to naturally replace the materials used to make the book you are holding.
Our forestry programme is run in accordance with the UK Woodland Assurance Scheme (UKWAS) and will be certified by the internationally recognized Forest Stewardship Council (FSC). The FSC is a non-government organization dedicated to promoting responsible management of the world's forests. Certification ensures forests are managed in an environmentally sustainable and socially responsible basis. For further information about this scheme, go to www.annesspublishing.com/trees

Previously published as part of a larger volume, *The Aztec and Maya World*

PICTURE ACKNOWLEDGEMENTS
Ancient Art and Architecture Collection Ltd: 5.5, 8t, 22b, 24t, 26l, 27b, 32t, 39t, 42b, 43, 52b, 61b, 73b, 74t, 77, 81t, 83b, 84b, 86–7, 92b, 97tl, 98b, 99b, 105b, 113t, 116t, 117t&b, 119b, 120t, 122b, 123b, 125b
Art Archive: 1, 88b, 114; /Antochiw Collection, Mexico/Mireille Vautier: 75t, 89t; /Archaeological Museum, Copan, Honduras/Dagli Orti: 79b; /Archaeological Museum, Teotihuacan, Mexico/Dagli Orti: 53; /Archaeological and Ethnological Museum, Guatemala City /Dagli Orti: 43, 83t, 102b; /Biblioteca Nacional, Madrid/Dagli Orti: 101t, 103t, 121; /Biblioteca Nacional, Mexico/ Dagli Orti: 19t, 67t, 78b; /Biblioteca Nacional, Mexico/Mireille Vautier: 19b, 104; /Bibliothèque de l'Assemblée Nationale, Paris/Dagli Orti: 79t, 100b, 109b; /Bodleian Library, Oxford: 46b, 54t, 59b, 65, 72, 91b, 94, 95t, 116b; /British Museum, London /Eileen Tweedy: 4, 99t; /Joseph Martin: 90b, 98tr; /Museo de America, Madrid/Dagli Orti: 96t; /Museo Ciudad, Mexico/Dagli Orti: 71; /Museo de Michoacan, Morelia, Mexico/ Dagli Orti 54b; /Museo del Popol Vuh, Guatemala/ Dagli Orti: 82b; /Museo Regional de Antropologia, Merida, Mexico/ Dagli Orti: 110t; /Museo Regional de Oaxaca, Mexico/Dagli Orti: 64r; /Museo del Templo Mayor, Mexico/Dagli Orti: 9b, 119t; /Museo de Teotenango, Mexico/ Dagli Orti: 102t; /Museum of Mankind, London /Eileen Tweedy: 58; /National Anthropological Museum, Mexico/Dagli Orti: 3, 21t, 24b, 26r, 50t, 73t, 75b, 95b, 96b, 97r, 103b, 105t, 108t, 115t, 122t, 124t, 125t; /National Archives, Mexico/ Mireille Vautier: 100t, 120b; /National Ethnological Museum, Mexico/ Dagli Orti: 76t; /Dagli Orti: 18t, 21b, 27t, 50b, 61t, 63, 67b, 76b, 80b, 84t, 89b, 111b; /Mireille Vautier: 5.4, 5bl, 6–7, 30t, 31b, 57t, 68–9, 70t, 74b, 115b; /Franceso Venturi: 59t; /Xalapa Museum, Veracruz, Mexico/Dagli Orti: 93, 108b.
Corbis: /Paul Almasy: 101b, 110b; /Artephot /Corbis Sygma: 118t; /Yann Arthus Bertrand: 20b; /Bettmann: 62b; /Macduff Everton 11t, 56b; /Werner Forman: 82t, 91t; /Arvind Garg: 17b; /Danny Lehman: 56t; /Charles and Josette Lenars: 123t; /North Carolina Museum of Art: 5.1, 12–13; /Gianni Dagli Orti: 81b; /Reuters; /Kevin Schafer: 111t.
South American Pictures: /Robert Francis: 2, 10tl&tr, 14t, 20t, 37t&b, 44b; /Tony Morrison: 5.2, 5.6, 14b, 15t, 28–9, 30b, 31t, 33b, 42t, 85b, 106–7; /Iain Pearson: 16t, 32b, 39b, 55b, 60t&b; /Chris Sharp: 5.3, 23b, 25t, 34t&b, 35t, 36, 38t&b, 40t, 41, 44t, 45t&b, 46t, 48–9, 51t&b, 56t, 57b, 62t, 64b, 66b, 70b, 80b, 85tr, 92t, 109t, 112t, 124b; /Kate Smith: 47t.

CONTENTS

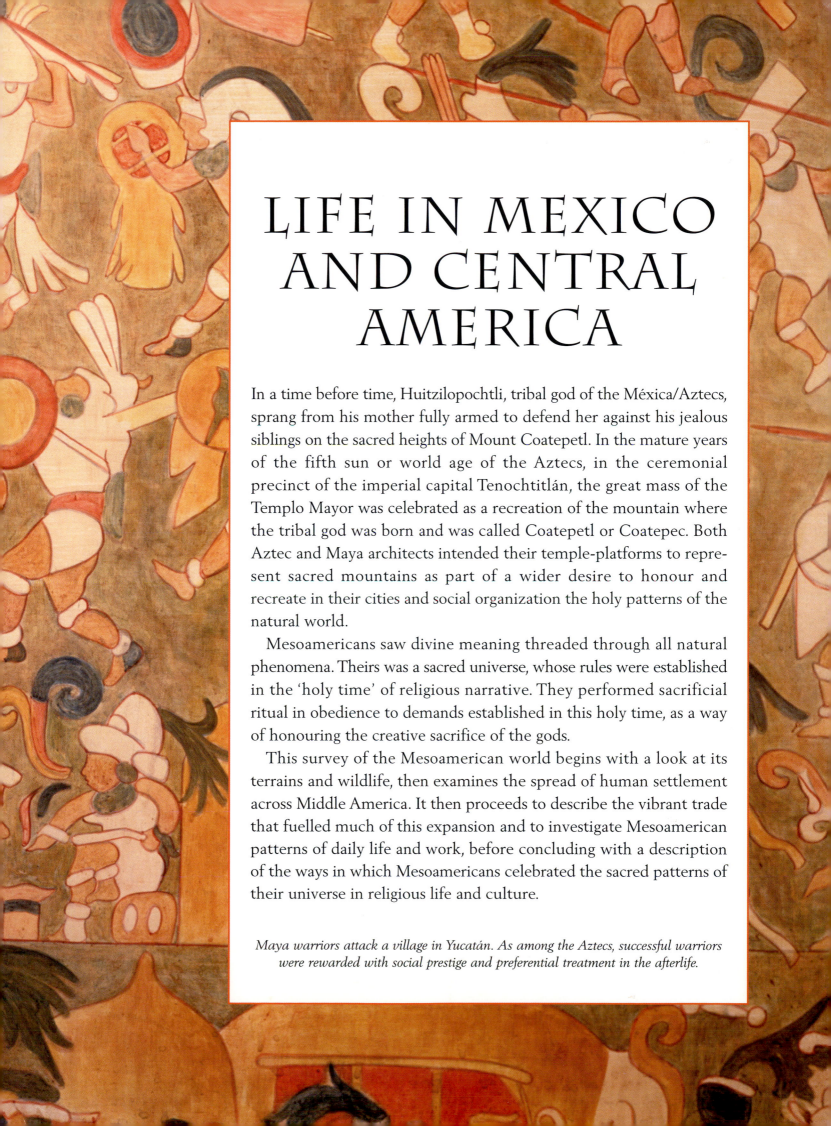

LIFE IN MEXICO AND CENTRAL AMERICA

In a time before time, Huitzilopochtli, tribal god of the México/Aztecs, sprang from his mother fully armed to defend her against his jealous siblings on the sacred heights of Mount Coatepetl. In the mature years of the fifth sun or world age of the Aztecs, in the ceremonial precinct of the imperial capital Tenochtitlán, the great mass of the Templo Mayor was celebrated as a recreation of the mountain where the tribal god was born and was called Coatepetl or Coatepec. Both Aztec and Maya architects intended their temple-platforms to represent sacred mountains as part of a wider desire to honour and recreate in their cities and social organization the holy patterns of the natural world.

Mesoamericans saw divine meaning threaded through all natural phenomena. Theirs was a sacred universe, whose rules were established in the 'holy time' of religious narrative. They performed sacrificial ritual in obedience to demands established in this holy time, as a way of honouring the creative sacrifice of the gods.

This survey of the Mesoamerican world begins with a look at its terrains and wildlife, then examines the spread of human settlement across Middle America. It then proceeds to describe the vibrant trade that fuelled much of this expansion and to investigate Mesoamerican patterns of daily life and work, before concluding with a description of the ways in which Mesoamericans celebrated the sacred patterns of their universe in religious life and culture.

Maya warriors attack a village in Yucatán. As among the Aztecs, successful warriors were rewarded with social prestige and preferential treatment in the afterlife.

INTRODUCTION

Human activity in the region of Mexico and neighbouring Guatemala dates back 20,000 years or more, to the time when the first hunter-gatherers settled in the area. Between that time and the height of the Aztec empire, in the 14th–16th centuries AD, a number of civilizations rose and fell in the locality.

MANY CIVILIZATIONS

Historians apply the name 'Meso-america' both to these civilizations and to the area in which they arose. This ran southwards from the desert regions of north-central Mexico, then eastwards to include the Isthmus of Tehuantepec, the Yucatán peninsula, Guatemala, Honduras, western Nicaragua and north-western Costa Rica. Among these civilizations were the Olmecs, carvers of magnificent stone monuments and creators of a vast trading network in the 2nd millennium BC; the Zapotecs, builders of a mountaintop settlement at Monte Albán

Below: Chacmools received offerings of human hearts. This chacmool stood before the temple to Tláloc in Tenochtitlán.

in Oaxaca, who may have been the first people in the region to develop written communication c.500BC; and the builders of the mysterious monumental city of Teotihuacán in highland Mexico c.100BC–c.AD500, who excelled in trade, the manufacture of enigmatic masks and the painting of evocative murals.

Others included the Maya, who in the period c.AD250–900 raised magnificent temples and palaces in the jungles of Guatemala and in parts of eastern Mexico, and who continued to thrive until the Spanish Conquest; the militaristic Toltecs, who built their capital Tollán north-west of Teotihuacán c.AD950 and developed bloodthirsty religious rites involving human sacrifice; the Mixtecs, who succeeded the Zapotecs in Oaxaca and who excelled in metalworking and hand-painted screenfold books; the Tarascans of Michoacán in western Mexico, highly skilled metalworkers who forged an empire after 1200; and the México, or Aztecs, who in the years after founding their capital of Tenochtitlán in 1325 built a vast empire encompassing 150,000sq km (58,000sq miles).

Above: A carving of an enigmatic quetzal-butterfly adorns the elegant Quetzalpapálotl Palace in Teotihuacán.

DUALITY AND CHANGE

The Mesoamericans' understanding that time moved in cycles governed by the gods was balanced by an acute awareness of patterns of change. The Aztecs and the Maya understood the universe to be structured according to a divinely ordained duality: life and death, day and night, light and darkness, wet and dry, the celestial realm and the underworld realm all balanced each another.

Day was followed by night, the rainy season alternated with the dry season, life was followed by death – and then by new life. A king's death was the prelude to his voyage to the underworld, land of the dead, and followed by his ascent to the celestial realm. However, the gods could break this sacred pattern of alternation at any time. Each night, the sun took the form of a jaguar and had to fight its way through the underworld before it could be reborn in the eastern sky. A day might come on which the gods withdrew their favour and the sun did not rise.

SIERRA MADRE ORIENTAL

La Quemada

HUASTECS

CHICHIMECS

METZTITLÁN

Tula/Tollán

El Tajín

Zacapu

Tenochtitlán

OTOMÍ

Teotihuacán

Cempoala

Tzintzuntzán

Tlaxcala

Calixtlahuaca

AZTECS

TLAXCALLÁN

TARASCANS

Cholula

TOTONACS

Potonchán

Teotenango

Tepoztlán

Tres Zapotes

Malinalco

TLAHUICAS

Yagul

San

Xochicalco

Chalcatzingo

Lorenzo

La Venta

Huaxtepec

Tilantongo

Monte Albán

Mitla

Xochipala

YOPITZINGO

MIXTECS

Tehuantepec

Gulf of Mexico

Dzibilchaltún Aké Chichén Itzá

Mayapán

Cobá

Maní

Yaxuná

Uxmal

Chumayel

Dzibilnocác

Edzná

MAYA STATES

Becán

Colhá

Tikal

Palenque

Yaxchilán

Bonampak

Yucatán Basin

Izapa

QUICHÉ STATES

Copán

SOCONUSCO

Kaminaljuyú

PACIFIC OCEAN

FATE AND FATALISM

Throughout Mesoamerica, astronomer-priests made observations of the cycles of the planets and the movements of the stars, while shaman-priests interpreted the intricate ritual calendars and also performed rites of divination using psychotropic substances.

Those who relied on the statements of these experts believed that the diviners had the power to identify sacred influences on human activity in the patterns of the sky and in the cycles of time. Some historians argue that beliefs in divination, the power of omens and the inevitability of time's repeating patterns made Mesoamericans more fatalistic than they would otherwise have been when faced with a challenge.

The so-called 'Maya collapse' – when in the 9th and 10th centuries AD a series of powerful cities across Guatemala stopped erecting dated monuments to

Above: Mesoamerican cultural sites ranged over the years from San Lorenzo to Tenochtitlán and over miles from Tikal to La Quemada.

the glory of their kings and fell into rapid decline – had many causes, most principally environmental degradation, but decline was possibly also encouraged by a fatalistic belief among some of the Maya that the decline could be predicted from the patterns of time, that, by the gods' choice, these events mirrored others many centuries earlier and so were not worth resisting.

Equally, there were many practical causes for the defeat of the mighty Aztec empire by a small band of Spanish invaders fighting in alliance with local peoples, but historical accounts reveal

Right: Aztec pilgrims took this greenstone mask from Teotihuacán and offered it in the Templo Mayor, Tenochtitlán.

that Aztec leaders were aware that the omens were bad and appeared to prophesy their downfall. Some in Tenochtitlán thought Cortés was destined for victory, and some Aztecs even believed that Cortés was the Mesoamerican god Quetzalcóatl making a long-promised return to claim his rightful inheritance in Tenochtitlán.

TIMELINE OF MESOAMERICA

PRECLASSIC PERIOD TO AD250

Above: Olmec stone heads may have been used in rites honouring royal ancestors.

3114BC The start date of the Maya Long Count dating system is equivalent to 13 August 3114BC.

2300BC Artist at Tlapacoya makes the oldest surviving ceramic figurine.

1400BC Oldest known ball court constructed at Paso de la Amada, Chiapas.

c.1400BC Potters in highland Mexico, fashion many ceramic figurines, probably for use as grave offerings.

1250–900BC Olmecs lay out pyramids and courts in their holy town of San Lorenzo.

1200BC Coapexco becomes a centre for the growing trade in obsidian.

1100BC Olmec influence seen in rock carvings at the trading centre of Chalcatzingo.

800–500BC Olmec stone heads set up in La Venta. Maya settlers build the pyramid Mound 30a at Izapa.

500BC The Zapotec city of Monte Albán is established in Oaxaca.

300BC Zapotec builders construct the main plaza of Monte Albán.

250BC Building of the North Acropolis begins at Tikal.

c.200BC Carvings of war prisoners added to Building L at Monte Albán.

200BC–AD300 Building J, an astronomical observatory and military conquest monument built at Monte Albán.

150BC–AD150 Vast El Tigre monument built in the Maya city of El Mirador.

100BC–AD150 Teotihuacán established as a sacred city and a major population centre. The Pyramid of the Sun is built and the Street of the Dead laid out.

31BC Stela C at Trez Zapotes, on the Mexican Gulf Coast, is carved with a date in the Maya Long Count equivalent to 3 September 31BC.

AD36 Stela 1 at El Baúl, Guatemala, is carved with a standing figure and the date AD36.

AD100 A ball court is built at Monte Albán.

AD156 Stela 1 at La Mojarra in Veracruz is carved with a standing figure and the dates AD143 and AD156.

c.AD200 The *talud-tablero* architectural feature is used on the Temple of the Feathered Serpent in Teotihuacán's Citadel area.

c.AD250 Artists decorate Teotihuacán temples with wall paintings.

C.AD250–900 CLASSIC PERIOD

Above: Tikal was a major city by AD300 and at its zenith in the 8th century AD.

AD300 The Zapotecs of Monte Albán establish the nearby settlement of Mitla, which contains many tombs. They call it Lyobaa ('Site of Burials').

AD400 Teotihuacáno influence is seen at the Maya site of Kaminaljuyú, where buildings begin to use the *talud-tablero* architectural feature.

AD426 The first ritual buildings are erected at Copán in the reign of King Yax Kuk Mo' (*r.* AD426–37).

AD647 King Pacal (*r.* AD615–83) begins a major building programme at the city of Palenque, with the construction of the Olvidado temple ('Unnoticed Shrine') to the west of the main plaza.

AD650 Potters at Remojadas and other sites in Veracruz produce ceramic figures for use in religious ritual.

AD692 At Palenque the temples of the Cross Group are dedicated.

c.AD700 El Tajín, in Veracruz, contains 12 ball courts and the remarkable Pyramid of the Niches, which contains 365 openings, one for each day of the solar year.

C.AD250–900 CLASSIC PERIOD

AD726 In Yaxchilán Lord Shield Jaguar (*r.* AD681–742) dedicates Temple 23 (Queen's House) to his wife, Lady Xoc.

AD734 Tikal's King Ah Cacau (*r.* AD682–734) buried beneath Temple I, which he built as his funerary monument.

AD738 King 18-Rabbit (*r.* AD695–78) completes building work on the Great Ball Court at Copán.

AD749 Copán's King Smoke Shell (*r.* AD749–763) completes the Hieroglyphic Stairway.

*c.*AD750 Builders erect Tikal's Temple VI (Temple of the Inscriptions) and the city's tallest building, Temple IV – 70m (230ft) tall.

*c.*AD750 Artists at Cacaxtla paint a series of magnificent murals.

AD775 At Copán, King Yax Pac (*r.* AD763–820) dedicates the monument known as Altar Q, which bears portraits of all 16 kings of the dynasty founded by Yax Kuk Mo'.

*c.*AD800 Tula/Tollán is laid out, like Teotihuacán, on a grid pattern.

*c.*AD900 Builders at Chichén Itzá erect the Caracol, perhaps as a temple to the wind god, but more likely as an astronomical observatory.

*c.*AD900 The Pyramid of the Feathered Serpent is built at Xochicalco.

POSTCLASSIC AND MODERN PERIODS AD900–2005

AD909 Monument 101 at Toniná is last carving with date in the Maya Long Count.

*c.*1230 The *Grolier Codex*, a calendar of the cycles of the planet Venus, is written.

*c.*1325 The México/Aztecs build the Templo Mayor in Tenochtitlán.

*c.*1345 The *Dresden Codex* is made.

*c.*1390 A larger pyramid-temple is constructed over the original Templo Mayor.

1431 The México/Aztecs build a third and much larger version of the Templo Mayor on the same site in Tenochtitlán.

1450–1500 A series of fine murals are painted in the Maya city of Tulum.

*c.*1450 The *Paris Codex* is compiled, perhaps in the Maya city of Mayapán.

1469 México/Aztec artisans carve a stone image of Coyolxauhqui to place at the foot of a staircase on the western face of the Templo Mayor pyramid.

22 Aug 1700 Death of Carlos de Siguenza y Gongora, Jesuit priest, pioneering historian and the first to lead archaeological investigations at Teotihuacán.

1746 Ruins of Palenque discovered.

May 1786 First archaeological investigations at Palenque.

1840 John Lloyd Stephens finds Quiriguá.

1848 First expedition to explore Tikal.

1853 Report on Tikal by Modesto Méndez published by Berlin Academy of Science.

Above: The first archaeological investigations at Palenque were in 1786.

1882 Sir Alfred Maudslay leads an official exploration of Yaxchilán.

1924–44 The Carnegie Institution (Washington DC) carries out an archaeological programme at Chichén Itzá.

1940–60 Acosta leads dig at Tula/Tollán.

1946 Giles Healey discovers Bonampak.

1971 Ancient sacred cave found beneath Pyramid of the Sun, Teotihuacán.

1978 Electrical worker discovers vast carving of Coyolxauhqui in Mexico City.

1997 'Codex' murals found at Mayapán.

1998 Archaeologists discover the oldest known Mesoamerican ball court at Paso de la Amada, Chiapas, *c.*1400BC.

2002 Guatemalan Maya jade artefacts found in an elite ceremonial burial at Teotihuacán's Pyramid of the Moon.

2003 Finds at San Andrés suggest the Olmec used a logographic writing system.

CHAPTER ONE

LAND OF DANGER AND REWARD

The Aztecs and Maya made their home in an unstable and unpredictable physical environment. They feared the sudden shiftings of the 'earth monster' when earthquakes struck. They dreaded the onset of drought, the tightening of the dry earth that squeezes life out of the withering crops. They were wary of the beasts of jungle and plain, not least the majestic jaguar; in coastal regions they fled the onslaught of hurricanes and violent storms.

They saw the gods and goddesses everywhere. Partly because the world could turn on them suddenly and destructively, they became convinced of the need to honour the gods. The Aztecs, following long-established Mesoamerican practice, believed that the cycle of the sun's morning birth following death at evening might suddenly stop if blood sacrifices to the gods were not maintained. Equally, Mesoamericans celebrated the gods for the glory of divine energy and the pattern of sacred meaning they saw in all things.

Life in Mesoamerica, lived in the presence of death and catastrophe, was keenly experienced. Mesoamericans entered an intense relationship with their land, a region of rich contrasts – from the mountains of highland Mexico to the plains of the Pacific and Gulf Coasts, from desert and semi-arid landscapes to river valleys, lake shores and the dense jungles of lowland Guatemala.

Left: Aztecs and Maya feared the anger of the region's many volcanoes. The oval crater of Popocatépetl has near-vertical sides. Poisonous volcanic gases erupt from vents in the walls.

HIGHLAND AND LOWLAND

Mesoamerica's first settlers in the second millennium BC could choose between living at sea level along estuaries rich in marine life, in well-watered lowland tropical forests teeming with animals or on dry, elevated plateaux surrounded by rocky uplands well provided with minerals and other resources. Their choice of altitude would largely have determined the climate they would have experienced.

ALTITUDE VARIATIONS

From sea level up to altitudes of about 900m (3,000ft), in lands dubbed *tierra caliente* ('hot territory'), average temperatures were high, with little seasonal variation. In these low-lying tropical regions today, the temperature variation between summer and winter months is generally as little as 5°C and winter is marked by the coming of the rains. In Veracruz, the region on the Gulf of Mexico where the Olmec civilization emerged in the second millennium BC,

Below: Pine forests occupy elevated tierra fria *('cold territory') beneath the peak of Nevado de Toluca, 4,577m (15,016ft) high.*

the average year-round daily temperature is 25°C (77°F). Average temperatures of 24–28°C (75–82°F) hold in the Yucatán peninsula, which was home to many northern Maya settlements.

At altitudes of 900–1,800m (3,000–6,000ft), in *tierra templada* ('temperate territory'), average temperatures are about 5°C lower. The mountaintop Zapotec city of Monte Albán sat at an altitude of 1,600m (5,200ft); average temperatures in the region today are around 18°C (64°F). At 1,800–3,400m (6,000–11,000ft) or *tierra fria* ('cold territory') an average temperature is 5°C or lower, with much greater seasonal variation than at higher altitude. Mexico City, which arose on the ruins of Aztec Tenochtitlán, lies at 2,300m (7,500ft) and has an average daily temperature of 15°C (59°F). Temperatures there can rise to 26°C (78°F) in the hottest month (May) and may fall to a low of 12°C (54°F) in the coldest month (January).

With experience, Mesoamericans discovered that the deep-coloured highland soils of the Valley of Mexico or the Valley of Oaxaca were extremely

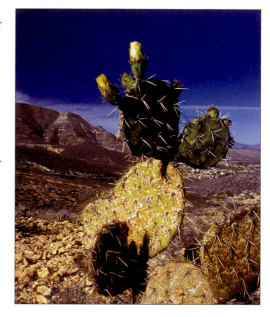

Above: Parched highlands such as this sweep of desert north of Chihuahua, Mexico, are typically rich in minerals.

mineral-rich and could be farmed intensively and on steep slopes. By comparison the earth in such lowland areas as El Petén in Guatemala often needed to be left fallow for prolonged periods to safeguard its fertility. Here farmers developed slash-and-burn agriculture, in which land was cleared with fire then used for perhaps three seasons before being left for as many as ten to recover its richness.

RAINFALL VARIATION

In parts of Mesoamerica drought was a persistent threat. Today, the Valley of Mexico receives as little as 600mm (23in) of rain in a year. However, other regions receive such abundant precipitation that they can support the vibrant growth of tropical rainforests. The Gulf coastal plain as far east as Tabasco, adjoining the Chiapas highlands, in whose foothills the great Maya city of Palenque arose, generally receives an annual average of 2,000mm (78in) of rain. To the southeast, in the jungle region of El Petén, average rainfall is around 1,350mm (53in) each year.

Above: Swamplands on the Mexican Gulf Coast made a resource-rich home for the earliest Mesoamerican settlers.

DROUGHTS OF THE 1450s

In the first years of rule by the Aztec *tlatoani* Moctezuma I (1440–69), a series of terrible calamities befell the peoples of the Valley of Mexico. In 1446 their harvests were lost to a plague of locusts, then in 1449 the island city of Tenochtitlán was flooded. Frosts and drought struck the crops for four consecutive years in 1450–4.

Chronicle accounts suggest that at the close of the 16th century – 150 years afterwards – people still told breathless tales of the privations of these times, when the weak and starving went hopelessly in search of food and watched with despairing eyes the circling shadows of vultures on the bone-dry ground. Sacrifices were urgently offered to the gods and finally, in 1455, the goggle-eyed rain god Tláloc returned with drenching rains. The people rejoiced in a bumper harvest of maize.

Across Mesoamerica the rainy season generally occurs between June and October. Rainfall can be very strong at the height of the season. Mexico City typically receives almost one third of its annual rainfall of 160mm (6in) in July alone, while Tabasco may be hit by 300mm (11in) in its wettest month (September). In El Petén the rainy season runs from June to December.

FLOODS AND HURRICANES

The Mesoamerican region was also vulnerable to storms, hurricanes and flooding. The Aztecs in their island city of Tenochtitlán were subject to periodic flooding, when the waters of Lake Texcoco rose with the spring rains. The east coast of Mexico adjoining the Gulf of Mexico and the eastern edge of the Yucatán peninsula frequently lay in the path of hurricanes. The Aztec god Tezcatlipoca had special power over hurricane winds, as did the Palenque god Tahil (Obsidian Mirror) and the Quiché Maya sky god Huracán.

The land was young: the great peaks of Citlaltépetl and Popocatépetl were recent outcrops in geological terms, having been driven upwards in the late Tertiary period (as little as 1.6 million years ago).

Mesoamericans must have felt deep respect for the untameable power of nature. They lived in one of the most dynamic areas of the Earth for volcanic and seismic activity and were familiar with the shudderings of the earth monster and the periodic explosions of the volcanoes that spotted the landscape.

Below: Tezcatlipoca, Lord of the Hurricane, was feared for his capricious nature. The Aztecs called him called Yáotl ('Adversary').

SACRED HEIGHTS

The Aztec territories in the Valley of Mexico are surrounded by mountains. The Aztecs and their forebears watched rain clouds gather around the great peaks before being blown by sweet winds to water the maize crops. Their priests taught that the rain god Tláloc stored his life-giving waters on the mountainsides and sent his assistants, the *tlaloques*, to gather the water and pass it to the lord of winds, Éhecatl-Quetzalcóatl. The great peak of Popocatépetl, part of the transverse volcanic axis that cuts across the southern part of the Mesa Central plateau, was sacred to Tláloc.

MOUNTAIN PERSONAE

Popocatépetl, whose name means 'Smoking Mountain' in the Aztecs' Nahuatl language, lies 72km (45 miles) to the south-east of the centre of Mexico City, in full view of the spot where the people of Tenochtitlán once raised their great temple pyramid to the glory of

Below: Popocatépetl is still an active volcano, belching smoke and gas as recently as 2000.

Tláloc and their patron deity Huitzilopochtli. Permanently snow-capped, it climbs to 5,465m (18,000ft), its height second only to Citlaltépetl (or Orizaba) in Mesoamerica. Offerings were made to Popocatépetl in Aztec times and shrines to Tláloc were built on its slopes. Popocatépetl remains active. The smoking peak erupted in 1947 and in 1994 it emitted a vast cloud of ash and gas that scientists feared was the prelude to another major eruption. It belched smoke and gas in 2000, but the volcano has since remained quiet.

The great mountain's twin, Ixtaccíhuatl ('White Lady' in Nahuatl), has three snow capped peaks that are said to resemble the head, feet and chest of a reclining woman. An Aztec folk tale cast Ixtaccíhuatl as a princess mourning the loss of her lover, who had been dispatched by her jealous father to a war in Oaxaca. The volcano is dormant.

The steep cone of Citlaltépetl ('Star Mountain'), Mexico's highest mountain, rises to 5,700m (18,700ft) about 80km (120 miles) to the east of Tenochtitlán

Above: A snow-covered plateau lies beneath one of the three peaks of Ixtaccíhuatl. Now dormant, the volcano last erupted in 1868.

and 40km (60 miles) from the Gulf of Mexico. The snowcapped peak of this volcano is also known as Pico de Orizaba. It held a significant place in Aztec religious narrative, for it was in the crater of Citlaltépetl that the revered prince-god Quetzalcóatl was said to have died after his retreat from the Toltec city of Tollán. He then reappeared in human form and departed into the Gulf of Mexico on a raft of snakes. An Aztec garrison named Ahuilzapán ('Pleasant Waters') lay at the foot of Citlaltépetl, on the site of the modern settlement of Orizaba. The volcano was active in Aztec times, but it has been dormant since 1687.

Another peak sacred to the Aztecs was Nevado de Toluca, Mexico's fourth-highest mountain, which rises to 4,577m (15,016ft) above the valley that bears its name to the west of Tenochtitlán. Nevado de Toluca was known as Xinantecatl in Nahuatl. Natural lakes in its dormant crater were used for religious rites and sacrificial offerings in Aztec times.

In the south-western Valley of Mexico rose the Xitle volcano, whose eruption in *c.*50BC devastated the developing ceremonial centre of Cuicuilco, at that time the arch-rival of Teotihuacán. Mesoamerican history in the Valley of

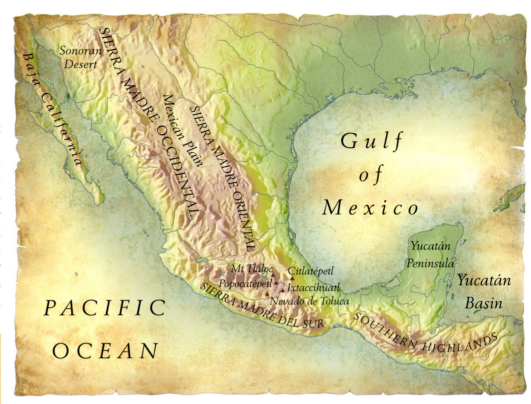

Mexico might have taken a very different course had this catastrophe not occurred, and ceremonial centres might have been flanked by round stepped pyramid-platforms like the one built at Cuicuilco rather than the square or rectangular platforms developed at Teotihuacán and elsewhere. The builders of Teotihuacán laid out their city to align with another very important Mexican peak, Cerro Gordo ('Fat Mountain'), which formed a

MYTHICAL PEAKS

Mountains play a key part in Aztec and Maya religious narratives. The Aztecs' tribal god Huitzilopochtli was born on the slopes of Mount Coatepetl (Serpent Mountain), while the Aztecs reported that they travelled to Culhuacán (Curving Mountain) on their southward migration from the barren north to the Valley of Mexico. The account of Huitzilopochtli's birth tells that his mother, the serpent-petticoated earth goddess Coatlícue, served as a priestess at a mountain shrine high on the slopes of Coatepetl.

Historians are agreed that this peak had no counterpart in reality, but report that the Aztecs applied the name Coatepetl or Coatepec to their great pyramid in Tenochtitlán, the Templo Mayor, which bore a shrine to Huitzilopochtli in its upper reaches. Culhuacán might also have been a mythical site, although some authorities have suggested a peak near the modern Mexican town of San Isidro Culhuacán as a possible location. An illustration in the *Historia Tolteca-Chichimeca* (1550–70) suggests that the curved mountain was also the setting of the seven sacred caves from which the Aztecs emerged, reborn from the earth, at a key point of their southward journey.

northern backdrop for the Pyramid of the Moon and the Street of the Dead. Cerro Gordo was itself the site of a temple and small ceremonial plaza.

MAYA MOUNTAINS

Large numbers of Maya lived far from mountains, in the jungled lowlands of El Petén or in the low-lying scrub of northern Yucatán. However, they shared the reverence of their Mesoamerican cousins for the sacred heights: the towering stone temples of cities such as Tikal were recreations in stone of the mountains that they believed were home to their ancestors after death. Sacred buildings such as those in Group E at Uaxactún were adorned with stucco masks signifying that they were holy mountains.

In the southern Maya territories of eastern Mexico and the southern highlands, which run from the border of the Chiapas region across Guatemala and into north-eastern Honduras, lay the mountains of the Sierra Madre de Chiapas. Of the Chiapas peaks, the volcano Tacana ('Fire House') rises to 4,050m (13,290ft).

The mountains of the southern highlands are mostly young and active volcanoes. The highest is the twin-peaked Tajumulco, which rises to 4,220m

Above: Four tectonic plates – Pacific, Cocos, Caribbean and North American – clash in Mesoamerica, pushing up great mountain chains and causing frequent earthquakes.

(13,845ft) and is dormant. In central Guatemala the extinct San Pedro volcano and the still active 3,535m (11,600ft) Atitlán volcano rise majestically above the waters of Lago Atitlán. The 3,158m (10,358ft) Toliman and the 3,763m (12,340ft) Fuego volcanoes, which are also in Guatemala, have been active as recently as 2002 and 2004 respectively.

Below: Beneath the Atitlán volcano in Guatemala, the waters of Lago Atitlán fill a large crater formed by volcanic subsidence.

LIFE-GIVING WATERS

The lakes of the Valley of Mexico were formed in prehistoric times when the sacred heights of Popocatépetl, Ixtaccíhuatl and other peaks of the transverse volcanic axis rose, damming the south-easterly drainage of the region's waters. Lake Texcoco, site of the Aztecs' island capital, was one of five expanses of water. It lay between lakes Zumpango and Xaltocán to the north and Xochimilco and Chalco to the south.

Lake Texcoco was the lowest of these in altitude. In the rainy summer season the other lakes would rise beyond their normal extent and flow into Lake Texcoco, creating one single expanse of water that the Aztecs dubbed Moon Lake. In the dry season, however, the two northern lakes, which lay 3.5–6m (11–19ft) higher in altitude than Lake Texcoco, would effectively disappear. The southern lakes of Xochimilco and Chalco,

Below: Mesoamerican rivers, notably the long Usumacinta in Yucatán/Guatemala, were major facilitators of trade.

3m (10ft) higher than Lake Texcoco, were fed by freshwater springs and remained, although they were separated from the central lake.

Scholars believe that farming using *chinampa* or artificial islands was pioneered in the Classic Period *c.*AD800 by the people of a settlement named Xico by Lake Chalco. By the time of the Aztec empire, Lakes Chalco and Xochimilco were the setting for great expanses of *chinampa* fields.

FROM HIGHLANDS TO SEA

To the west of the Valley of Mexico, the Lerma river rises in the region of Nevado de Toluca and flows north-westward to create Lake Chapala. From here, the Santiago river flows south down across the Sierra Madre Occidental into the Pacific Ocean. To the south of the Valley of Mexico the major river is the Balsas, which runs west into the Pacific Ocean and gives it name to the low-lying region known as the Balsas Depression. A second waterway, the Papaloapan, flows

Above: The Sacred Cenote *at Chichén Itzá is around 30m (100ft) across. There is a drop of 22m (70ft) from the rim.*

at a stately pace eastward into the Gulf of Mexico. Archaeologists believe that it was in fertile lands near the Balsas that early Mesoamerican farmers succeeded in domesticating maize from the wild grass known as *teosinte*.

To the east, beyond the low-lying Isthmus of Tehuantepec, the major rivers are the Usumacinta and the Grijalva, which together drain the waters of the Chiapas highlands. The Grijalva forms from headstreams that arise in the Sierra de Soconusco in Mexico and the Sierra Madre of Guatemala. It flows in a north-westerly direction through the state of Chiapas. The Usumacinta, formed in the Chiapas highlands by the combination of the Pasión and Chixoy rivers of Guatemala, flows north-westward towards the region of Tabasco and the Bay of Campeche. One of its three branches combines with the Grijalva before flowing into the Bay of Campeche near the modern town of Frontera, while a second, now called the San Pedro y San Pablo, feeds into the bay near the settlement of San Pedro. A third, now known as the Palizada, flows into the Términos Lagoon in the state of Campeche. The Usumacinta was an important 1,000km (600 mile) trading route.

WATERWAYS AND SETTLEMENT

Several important Maya settlements grew up close to these waterways. The ceremonial centre known as Altar de Sacrificios was founded at the very point where the Pasión and Chixoy rivers join to form the Usumacinta. A carved stela of AD455 shows the site was occupied in the early-to-mid Classic Period, while later evidence shows that it reached a peak of prosperity after AD600 for around two centuries. Farther west, Bonampak was built on the banks of the small Lacanja river. Around 80km (50 miles) down the Usumacinta from Altar de Sacrificios, Yaxchilán was founded on a terrace overlooking the river after AD300. A further 50km (30 miles) downstream, the Maya city of Piedras Negras was built on a hill in a bend of the Usumacinta. Still farther north-west, Palenque was built on the Otulum River, a small tributary of the Usumacinta, and overlooking the Usumacinta floodplain that runs down to the Bay of Campeche.

In the south-eastern Maya region the river Motagua rises in the central Guatemalan highlands in the region occupied by the Quiché Maya and runs for 400km (250 miles) eastwards to empty into the Gulf of Honduras. It was a major route for trade moving from highland Guatemala to the Caribbean. The Maya city of Quiriguá was established

close to the river by the 5th century AD. Copán drew much of its wealth from trade in obsidian and other natural resources on this river before it lost control of the trade to Quiriguá in AD738.

UNDERGROUND WATERS

On the Yucatán peninsula of Mexico, towards the northern edge of the Maya realm, there are no significant rivers. Rainfall drains away underground through porous limestone rock and there are very few surface streams. In places, this rock collapses to expose underground stores

Above: This drawing of the Bolonchen cenote is from Incidents of Travel in Central America, Chiapas and Yucatán *(1841).*

of water in natural wells named *cenotes* – from the Yucatec term *dz'onot. Cenotes* can be very large, measuring up to 60m (200ft) across and 30m (100ft) deep. There are around 6,000 *cenotes* in north-eastern Yucatán.

Cenotes were important sources of water for the Maya. They were also used for religious sacrifice and were understood to be entrances to the underworld. Of the two *cenotes* at Chichén Itzá, one was reserved for religious offerings and one was used for water supply. *Cenotes* were sacred to the rain god Chac.

Left: The Aztecs held the waters of lakes, rivers and sea sacred to Chalchiúhtlicue. This image is from the Codex Vaticanus.

TOWERING TREES, ROCKY SANDS

Many Maya made their living among dense jungle forests, tracking game or the rare quetzal bird, cutting back and burning the dense growth to fashion fields to grow crops and raising great stone temples that rivalled the height of the towering jungle trees. The wide variety of terrains, altitudes and climates encompassed by the Maya territories produced a range of distinct forests.

In the Alta Verapaz of Guatemala, at the northern edge of the southern Maya highlands, stand the highland rainforests, home of the rare and sacred quetzal, whose brightly coloured tail feathers were a valued item of trade among the Maya and other Mesoamericans. These humid

Below: The partly ruined Nohuch Mul pyramid rises 24m (80ft) to imitate a natural mountain at the Maya city of Cobá.

greenlands, sometimes called cloud forests, are dense with tropical growth of evergreens, lichens and mosses, delicate wild orchids, bromeliads and astonishing ferns that reach a height of 15m (50ft). Here professional hunters would track the quetzal in order to capture it alive, pluck its wondrous tail feathers and then set it free once more. In the wild the bird would grow new feathers after moulting.

STOREYED FOREST LIFE

In the lower altitude and denser rainforests of the southern Maya lowlands, different types of plant life thrive at distinct levels above ground. At the topmost level, perhaps 70m (230ft) above ground, towering mahogany and ceiba, a form of cottonwood, predominate. At a lower level, up to 50m (165ft) above ground, Spanish cedar, sapodilla, bari and

Above: The Lacandón rainforest in Chiapas, an ancient Maya homeland, is today under threat from farmers and loggers.

American fig trees grow densely. A third level, at up to 25m (80ft) in height, is vibrant with palms, avocado trees, rubber trees, breadnut trees and others. Vines, bromeliads and lianas climb their trunks. Beneath, at ground level, in dense shade, young trees and ferns are found.

TREE OF LIFE

The majestic ceiba, or silk-cotton tree, was sacred to the Maya and identified by them as the cosmic tree or tree of life. They believed that it linked the levels of the universe, sinking its roots through the earth to the lowest of the nine levels of the underworld and sending its towering branches to the topmost of the 13 levels of heaven. In some versions of their cosmology, the Maya told that five great trees supported the heavens, one in each of the four points of the compass and a fifth, the green ceiba, in the centre.

The vines that hang far down from the great ceiba's branches may have symbolized a spirit voyage from the ground level of earthly reality to the heights of heaven in the tree's great umbrella-shaped canopy. There, far above the forest floor, both epiphytes (aerial plants) and many species of animal make their home;

Above: Dry lands. Hunters cross a stretch of desert in a detail from the Mapa Tlotzin, *a genealogy of the governors of Texcoco.*

birds nest, mammals move about along the great branches, even frogs raise their young in the pools that form on branches and in tree trunks.

The ceiba blooms in the evening, producing tiny flowers very reminiscent of the ear flares worn by kings in Maya carving and ceramic images. Some authorities suggest that the king dressed himself as the silk-cotton tree, to signify that he was blessed like the holy ceiba and that he anchored the kingdom in sacred order. The carving on the lid of the sarcophagus in which King Pacal of Palenque was interred shows the king descending into the spirit realm of the underworld along the length of the cosmic tree. The Maya carved great canoes from the vast trunk of their sacred tree.

SEASONAL RAINFOREST
Farther north, in the region known as the central lowlands, the jungle is described as 'seasonal rainforest' because each year extended dry periods interrupt the supply of rainwater. The upper canopy of American fig, ceiba and mahogany is lower and often less complete, but still climbs to 50m (165ft) above ground. Beneath, a thick growth of fig, sapodilla and other trees form a very dense canopy, while lower still, at a height of around

10m (30ft), palms, allspice and other species predominate. The growth of ferns and young trees at ground level is less vibrant here than further south. Here and there the forest gives way to seasonal swamps and grasslands. Tikal, Uaxactún, El Mirador and Calakmul all arose to glory in the central lowlands.

A PLACE OF NO CULTURE
At the other extreme of Mesoamerican terrains lay arid or semi-arid regions such as the wide plateau where the Toltec capital of Tollán was founded in highland Mexico and regions in Guatemala such as the Motagua Valley in the Maya highlands. In such areas the cult of the rain god was prominent and knowledge of irrigation techniques was key to agricultural success. Desert lay to the north in the northern part of the Mexican plateau, a region characterized by the Aztecs and their fellow inhabitants of the Valley of Mexico as a place of no culture, the place from which they had escaped in moving south. In the *Historia Tolteca Chichimeca*, an image of the seven caves from which the tribes were said to have emerged depicts several types of cacti, indicating that the primal landscape of origin in the first days was a sunblasted desert.

Below: At Labná in Yucatán, trees crowd close to the palace arch. To either side are stone representations of Maya village huts.

LIFE IN THE WILD

The lands of the Aztecs and Maya were teeming with animal life. Mesoamericans so revered these creatures for their energy and marvellous abilities that they cast many of them in religious and creation narratives and even saw some, such as the jaguar and eagle, as principal physical forms of great gods.

KING JAGUAR

Throughout the region, the jaguar was king. The largest member of the *felidae* family of cats, the jaguar (*Felis onca*) can thrive in scrubland and desert as well as in its preferred habitat of dense forests and swamps. It can climb with ease and track prey along branches tens of metres above ground, but is also happy to leap into water and is a strong swimmer. The male, which is significantly larger than the female, can grow to 2.7m (9ft) in length and weigh up to 160kg (350lbs.) The jaguar hunts alone. It prefers to stalk

Below: Bird sacred to Huitzilopochtli. This detail of a stone carving on the Platform of the Jaguars and Eagles at Chichén Itzá depicts an eagle eating a human heart.

peccaries (pig-like mammals) and the capybara (a large rodent), but will also kill and eat deer, sloths, monkeys, anteaters, alligators, birds, turtles and even fish. The jaguar does not usually attack humans, unless cornered, when it is a savage opponent.

The jaguar played an important role in Mesoamerican religious life from early times. In the second millennium BC, Olmec craftsmen were carving intriguing jaguar-faced figures resembling human babies. The jaguar was associated with the ancient practice of shamanism (spirit travel) and was adopted by shamans as one of their animal forms.

Because of its fearsome capacity to hunt in darkness, it was an animal aspect of Tezcatlipoca, the Aztec lord of night and of dark fate, while elsewhere in Mesoamerica it was associated with the god of the underworld and with the realm of darkness. When the sun visited the underworld by night, it took the form of the jaguar. Like the lion in Europe, the jaguar became a symbol of royalty and bravery in Mesoamerica: Maya kings wore its pelt and were named after the jaguar, while in the Aztec army the two elite groups of fighters were called eagle and jaguar warriors.

The Aztecs called the jaguar *océlotl*. The smaller cat now known as the ocelot was known to the Aztecs as the *tlacaoocélotl* (literally, 'little jaguar'; *Felis pardalis*).

HUNTING ANIMALS AND BIRDS

When Mesoamericans went hunting they most commonly killed rabbits and white-tailed deer. Rabbits, perhaps because of their skittering speed of movement and rapid rate of reproduction, were associated by the Aztecs with drunkenness and with the alcoholic drink *pulque*. Maya and Aztec people also killed and ate ducks, geese, swans and other birds. The Hero Twins of Mayan mythology were celebrated for their skill in hunting birds using blowpipes.

Above: Ocelots, known to the Aztecs as 'little jaguars', were common in the fertile lowlands of Mesoamerica along with opossums and tapirs.

Mesoamericans also hunted the rare quetzal bird, which was tracked and captured for its magnificent tail plumes, but never killed. The quetzal is found in the highland cloud forests that run from Chiapas to western Panama. Just 35cm (14in) long, it has tail feathers of up to 1m (3ft 3in) in length. These plumes change colour in the light, a shimmer of gold, emerald green and blue that sets off the bird's bright red breast.

Only the male bird possesses the iridescent tail feathers that are so highly prized: as with the peacock and peahen, the female bird is much plainer in appearance. The quetzal was an animal form of the great Plumed Serpent

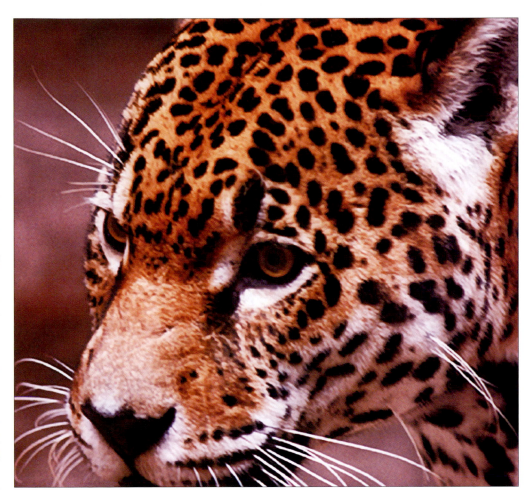

Quetzalcóatl and the feathers of the sacred bird were, like the jaguar pelt, symbolic of kingly authority.

Probably the most revered of birds was the eagle. An animal form taken by the Aztecs' tribal god Huitzilopochtli, it was central to Aztec origin narrative: the México/Aztecs founded their city of Tenochtitlán at the place where they saw an eagle destroying a snake upon a cactus, in fulfilment of a prophecy of Huitzilopochtli. The harpy eagle was found in the jungles of Maya lands while the golden eagle was known in central Mexico.

Other notable birds included parrots, macaws and toucans, falcons, owls, hawks and other birds of prey and, in estuaries and along coastlines, herons, giant storks and egrets. In the *Popol Vuh* of the Quiché Maya, the scarlet macaw, a vividly coloured species of parrot, attempted to set himself up as the pre-eminent god and to take the place of the sun, but he was outwitted by the Hero Twins. The hummingbird was another bird associated with Huitzilopochtli by the Aztecs.

BATS
The bat was also widely found. In the jungle bats nested beneath the vast roots of the ceiba that was viewed as the tree of life and understood to link the earth with the underworld and the heavens. Partly for this reason, and partly because of their natural associations with darkness, bats were linked to the underworld. The Zapotecs of Monte Albán associated the bat god with maize and fertility.

SNAKES AND MONKEYS
The snake was a complex and central religious symbol, associated with Tláloc and the rain, with the fertility of the earth, with the sun and heavens, with sacrificial blood and with religious and visionary experience. Mesoamericans also revered turtles and crocodiles: they sometimes said that the earth took the form of a crocodile or was resting on the back of a giant turtle. The Maya also identified the constellation Orion as a celestial turtle.

Monkeys were common in the lowlands. Species included howlers, spider monkeys and marmosets. Howlers, stocky, bearded monkeys up to 70cm (28in) long, live mainly in the upper branches of trees and would rarely have been seen. However, they would certainly have been heard: they take their name from the extremely resonant howl that they emit at dawn and dusk and during storms. The howler's cry can be heard more than 5km (as much as 3 miles) away. Marmosets are small, long-tailed monkeys that move quickly along branches, while spider monkeys are much larger with pot bellies. They forage in small groups among the very highest jungle branches. They rarely descend to the ground, but can be seen leaping from one tree to another. The Quiché Maya creators of the *Popul Vuh* narrative, which imagines a series of failed creations before the current one, told that monkeys were the descendants of a failed race of wooden people fashioned in early days by the creators.

Above: The jaguar is the largest New World cat. Like the lion in Europe, it became a symbol of royalty and bravery in Mexico.

Below: The intricate decoration in the Nunnery Quadrangle, Uxmal, contains twin images of the sacred rattlesnake.

FRUITS OF THE EARTH

The first humans in Mesoamerica were hunter-gatherers who survived on a diet of seeds and plants supplemented both by mammoths and mastodons and by smaller game, birds and fish. They lived in this way for many millennia before beginning to domesticate plants such as avocados, squash, beans and chilli peppers and turning to a settled, agricultural way of life.

PEOPLE OF MAIZE
The plant that would become their descendants' staple food – maize – was probably first domesticated from a wild cereal grass called *teosinte*. Archaeological evidence from the Tehuacán Valley in the Puebla region to the south-east of the Valley of Mexico suggests that, in the wild, the grass produced cobs that were no more than 2.5cm (1in) long: at this size, they could be an addition to a diet but not a staple food. In domesticating the plant, the first Mesoamerican farmers

Below: Images of the revered maize plant were carved on the sides of this basalt block used as an altar by the Aztecs.

succeeded in enlarging the cobs. In the wild, beans and squash grew alongside *teosinte* and other grasses, climbing up the grass stalks in the protection of the shade provided by the leaves. The first farmers, who had already domesticated varieties of squash and beans, might have copied this method of planting.

Archaeologists report that the first cereal domesticated in Mesoamerica was not *teosinte* but another, related to modern grain millet (*Setaria geniculata*). *Teosinte* itself was probably first domesticated in the lands adjoining the Balsas river of western Mexico some centuries before 5000BC. From archaeological remains we know that its use spread slowly eastwards, reaching the Tehuacán Valley by *c*.5000BC, Oaxaca by *c*.4000BC and Veracruz by *c*.2250BC. Its first cultivators perfected the making of stone mortars and used them to grind the maize ears.

Mesoamericans saw themselves as people reliant on, dedicated to and even made of maize. The word used by the Aztecs for the maize dough from which

Above: Xilonen, the Aztec goddess of young maize cobs, was worshipped in the form of a virginal adolescent girl.

they made tortillas is *toneuhcayotl* ('our flesh'). In some versions of both Maya and Aztec creation narratives, the first people were fashioned from a soft maize dough. In the *Popol Vuh*, the creators Huracán and Gucumatz gave ears of maize to a grandmother goddess Xmucané who ground them to flour, made a paste by mixing it with water and then moulded the first people.

According to Maya folk tradition, the first Mesoamericans were led to identify *teosinte* as a food source when they saw its grains in the dung of a wild cat. The *Popol Vuh* also recorded this debt to animals: Huracán and Gucumatz were led to the discovery of maize by four corn-eating creatures – a coyote, a fox, a parrot and a crow – who had tasted the maize

THE SEARCH FOR FOOD

Mesoamerican creation narratives proposed that before the current world age began there were a number of previous creations. The Aztec account of the five suns or world ages revealed that in each of the five creations the earth's inhabitants found a more satisfactory staple food than eaten by their predecessors.

In the era of the first sun, which was governed by Black Tezcatlipoca, the world was inhabited by a race of giants who lived on acorns. The second sun, whose presiding god was Quetzalcóatl, saw the emergence of a race of primitive humans who lived on the seeds of the mesquite tree.

After the third age, which was ruled by Tláloc, in which people lived on plants that grew on water, such as the water lily, people returned to a diet of wild seeds in the fourth age of Chalchiúhtlicue. It was only in the fifth and current age, an age subject to the sun god Tonatiuh, that the peoples of Mesoamerica learned how to plant and harvest maize.

Above: In a detail from one of the murals in Building A at Cacaxtla, a bird swoops to seize a cocoa pod from a sturdy cacao tree.

and found it good. In Aztec religious narratives, the god Quetzalcóatl – in some accounts, also a culture hero who taught people how to sow and harvest crops – discovered maize deep in the heart of a mountain, where it had been hidden by ants. He was unable to split the mountain to bring the maize to humans, but the god Nanahuatzin – who at the beginning of the current world age rose in the sky to become the sun – broke the peak apart with a thunderbolt.

FIELD AGRICULTURE

Mesoamericans developed different methods of field agriculture in the varied parts of their region. In arid and semi-arid areas fields were laid out where they could be watered by diverted springs and rivers, while in the region of Lake Texcoco farmers developed the technique of building *chinampa*, artificial islands, to reclaim land from the lake. In the dense jungles of the lowlands, fields were cut and the soil enriched by burning vegetation, while in the highlands further south, terraces were carved from the steep slopes.

By 1300BC, the four foods that would become the staple plants of the Mesoamerican civilization were well established in the fields of the pioneer farmers. Together they provided a balanced diet: carbohydrates from maize, protein from beans and squash, oils and fats from avocado. They could be supplemented with meat from rabbits, deer, ducks and geese and with fish.

Below: Cocoa beans are found within cocoa pods, the fruit of the cacao tree. The pods grow on the tree trunk and branches.

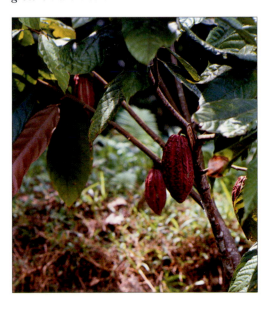

CREATING A SACRED WORLD

The oldest religion in Mesoamerica was the cult of the earth's fertility. At the very beginnings of settled life in central America, settlers were fashioning clay female figurines, believed to be representations of an archaic fertility goddess.

MOTHER AND MONSTER

From prehistoric times, Mesoamericans revered the earth as a mother with the capacity to gestate the seeds of domesticated plants and bring forth food. The ancient 260-day ritual calendar celebrated a sacred timespan that was possibly derived from both the lapse between planting and harvest in the Mesoamerican agricultural cycle and the time from conception to

Below: The duality of life and death is represented in a man/skeleton figure made by an Olmec craftsman c.500BC.

birth in a human pregnancy. The earth was a mother, but also a monster. In Aztec religious narrative, the earth monster Tlatecuhtli spread terror in the first days of the current era, when there was nothing but water. She was tamed by the gods Quetzalcóatl and Tezcatlipoca who tore her in two, making the sky from one half and the earth from the other.

OPPOSITES IN BALANCE

Mesoamericans believed the universe to be patterned by duality. Tlatecuhtli consumed the sun god each dusk, consigning him to the underworld for the hours of darkness, but the earth mother then gave birth to the sun once more in the redness of dawn. The earth goddess gave life in the form of crops but also demanded life in the form of sacrificial blood. Mesoamericans saw opposites held in balance. Darkness balancing light, death opposing life, dampness countering dryness, weakness balancing strength.

Duality also structured the divine sphere and was the hidden power of creation. The primal Aztec god Ometeotl ('Lord of Duality') took twin male and female forms, as Tonacatecuhtli ('Lord of our Sustenance') and Tonacacíhuatl ('Lady of our Sustenance') joined in a creative embrace. In Quiché Maya creation narrative, the earth was made when two gods, the sky god Huracán and the sea god Gucumatz came together in discussion. The gods had both benign and threatening aspects: the Maya rain god Chac or the Aztec rain deity Tláloc could deliver drought or lifegiving waters, destructive storms as well as the light moisture falling gently on crops.

The gods also had both spirit forms and physical forms, and most had animal aspects: Mesoamericans viewed the many powerful creatures of their landscape with deep reverence. In one version of the Aztec religious narrative

describing the creation of the sun and moon, the assembled gods who gave of their own blood to set the sun in motion afterwards became the animals of the plains, hills and jungles. The earth was opposed by the heavens, and also balanced the underworld.

In the Mesoamerican vision, the flat earth was both the lowest of the thirteen levels of heaven and the topmost of the nine levels of the underworld. The earth also gave access to the spirit realms of the underworld – the land was marked with sacred caverns that opened the way. The earth was also associated with snakes. According to the Maya, those in a state of religious ecstasy might be delivered

Below: The eagle, symbol of the god Huitzilopochtli and of warrior might, is celebrated on an Aztec wooden drum.

Above: Zoomorph P at Quiriguá shows a young ruler in the jaws of a monster, representing the entry to the underworld.

into the presence of ancestors or the gods by following the coils of a great snake known as the Vision Serpent.

SACRED PATTERNS

For Mesoamericans, the universe was structured according to sacred patterning. One of the forms of this patterning was that of the cyclical movement of time. Mesoamericans believed that everything happened in regular, periodic timespans. For this reason they structured their lives and religious ceremonies around the 260-, 365- and 584-day cycles of the moon, the sun and the planet Venus. Both the Maya and the Aztecs saw the current world as one of a series of creations, subject to periodic destruction and renewal.

In the Aztec view, the present age was the fifth sun or era, and this fivefold pattern was seen also in that of the five directions on the flat earth – north, south, east, west and the centre. In the centre was the great cosmic ceiba tree, and – for the Aztecs – the Templo Mayor of Tenochtitlán. The earth itself was also the centre point of creation, for Mesoamericans believed the earth to be surrounded by water. This gave sacred meaning to the island setting of the Aztecs' imperial capital of Tenochtitlán. The physical characteristics of Mesoamerica informed the range of associations that clustered around the directions of north and south.

To the north of the Valley of Mexico lay desert lands, inhospitable regions from which many nomads, including the Méxica/Aztecs, had escaped. The Aztecs saw the north as a place of dryness and death. It was the direction of the lord of deception and fate, Tezcatlipoca, and was linked to his colour, black – the hue of death. It was associated with xerophyte plants such as the Joshua tree that are adapted to desert climates. In the opposite direction, the south was said by the Aztecs to be the land of dampness, and of their tribal lord Huitzilopochtli, master of the arts of war through which they gathered sacrificial victims. In some versions, the south was the land of the rain god Tláloc, and like his heaven Tlálocan, a place of ease and lifegiving waters.

North and south appear to have been pre-eminent among the four directions. From at least Olmec times in the second millennium BC, many Mesoamerican sites were laid out on a roughly north–south plan. The same pattern was applied in Maya cities such as Tikal and Copán. For the Maya, north was the direction of the celestial realm, home of the gods, and south the way to the underworld. East and west were associated with the daily path of the sun.

Above the earth was the sacred sky, home of the sun god to whom the Aztecs, the people of the sun, dedicated themselves. By night, the movements of the stars followed paths established by the gods in religious and creation narrative. For example, the Great Bear constellation was identified with Tezcatlipoca and its dipping into the sea re-enacted the moment during his struggle with the earth monster at which he lost a foot. The cycle of the planet Venus eternally celebrated the achievements of the Aztec god Quetzalcóatl or the Maya Hero Twins in confronting the lords of the underworld.

In the sacred arenas of their cities, Mesoamericans created idealized versions of their world. Stone pyramids stood for mountains, wide plazas for lakes. Carved stone stelae – known to the Maya as stone trees – honoured the great trunks of the forest. Many scholars believe that the ball court was like a sacred cavern.

Below: This tiny Olmec female figurine was one of many Preclassic Period figures thought to have been used in fertility cults.

CHAPTER TWO

FROM VILLAGE TO METROPOLIS

In the great northern Yucatán city of Chichén Itzá, probably in the 9th–10th century or a little later, labourers raised the Temple of the Warriors, a four-level pyramid with a wide central stairway leading to a *chacmool* sacrificial figure and beyond it a square *cella* or temple. This awe-inspiring sacred building appears to be a copy of or tribute to the main pyramid-temple at Tollán in highland Mexico, the capital of the revered Toltecs. At one time scholars thought that Toltecs conquered Chichén Itzá, but most now agree that Toltec architectural features are present in the Yucatán city as a result of the peaceful spread of Toltec influence.

The debate over Chichén Itzá is typical of the many difficulties in tracing patterns of influence through Mesoamerican history. In attempting to make sense of the spread of settlements, we will rely on the conventional division of the region's history introduced elsewhere in this book, into the Preclassic Period (20,000BC–AD250), the Classic Period (*c.*AD250–AD900) and the Postclassic Period (AD900–1521). This tripartite division is certainly useful but the labels must not be applied too rigidly, for the divisions can fall at different chronological points in different areas of Mesoamerica: for example, in Belize and arguably northern Yucatán, historians agree that the Classic Period continues past AD900 until as late as 1200.

Left: The Great Plaza was the heart of the mountain-top settlement of Monte Albán, one of Mesoamerica's first cities.

THE BEGINNINGS OF SETTLED LIFE
7000–2000BC

In Mesoamerica, hunter-gatherer bands of humans first began to domesticate wild plants c.7000BC. Over 5,000 years they gradually became more successful at growing crops, little by little abandoning their nomadic pattern of existence and establishing permanent settlements, which were supported mainly by farming. Archaeological evidence suggests that the first settlements were established in two areas of Mesoamerica – in highland Mexico and along the coasts of the Gulf of Mexico, the Gulf of Tehuantepec and the Caribbean. Archaeologists suspect that in other areas, such as the central Maya region, people may have been following the same long, slow path from nomadic life to settled farming at the same time but the evidence has not been found in these places.

BEFORE FARMING
The evidence from highland Mexico shows that before humans first experimented with domesticating plants they were living as nomads in small bands of up to eight, hunting, trapping and gathering. They hunted species of antelope and horse that are now extinct, as well as rabbits, rats, birds, gophers and turtles. They used knives and sharpened points of chipped flint. They sometimes

Right: Mesoamerica's first hunter-gatherers trapped birds and other prey. This Totonac stone axe-shaped head is from after AD900.

drove mammoths and other large creatures into marshy land, where they killed them with sharpened flints. Archaeological finds show that two mammoths were killed in this way at the edge of Lake Texcoco in the Valley of Mexico some time around 7700BC.

THE FIRST CROPS
Over the following two millennia, c.7000–5000BC, the nomads of highland Mexico began to domesticate avocados, chillis and squash. They also ate the black seeds of a weed called amaranth, which were probably gathered in the wild, and chewed a wild cereal grass named *teosinte* that would become the staple food of Mesoamerica in the form of maize.

In this period, humans were living in the Tehuacán Valley in the south-eastern part of modern Puebla province, at an altitude of around 1,400m (4,600ft). They made milling stones as well as mortars and pestles and began to experiment with

weaving and woodworking. Groups settled in seasonal camps, but in spring left on nomadic trips. They killed cottontail rabbits and deer for meat. They buried skulls in baskets – perhaps as a rite of human sacrifice.

People were also living in the Infiernillo complex of caves in a desert environment in the south-western part of modern Tamaulipas province. They made fire-sticks, traps, rods and darts from wood and pioneered the making of mats and bags from yucca and agave plants. They ate wild runner beans, agave and prickly pear cactus and domesticated the bottle gourd and the chilli pepper.

At the same time, people in the Balsas region of western Mexico succeeded in domesticating *teosinte*. Another group made their living in caves near Mitla in Oaxaca. Like their cousins elsewhere, they hunted cottontail rabbits and deer, made flint tools and weapons and experimented with domesticating squash.

In 5000–3400BC, the inhabitants of the Tehuacán Valley began to establish semi-permanent camps that they inhabited for parts of the year, probably splitting into smaller nomadic groups only in the dry season. They succeeded in domesticating more plants, including *teosinte*, as well as

Left: From early days, Mesoamericans made alcoholic drinks from the maguey agave plant, which grew in Oaxaca.

the common bean, the crookneck squash and the bottle gourd. They cultivated sapotes, plum or apple-sized fruits with a sweet flavour. At another site in Oaxaca, Gheo-Shih, people were living in a semi-permanent site through summer and autumn, hunting but also raising maize.

From 3400 to 2000BC, the people of the Tehuacán Valley built larger settlements on river terraces they probably occupied all year round. They domesticated new plants, including the pumpkin, and began to keep and eat dogs. They made bowls from stone and long blades of obsidian. They trapped small animals such as foxes, turtles and birds rather than larger creatures such as puma or deer. However, as before, some members set off in nomadic hunting groups during the dry season and left evidence of their passing in highland caves.

A LAKESIDE HOME
In the more fertile setting of Lake Chalco in the Valley of Mexico, people began to live in permanent settlements much earlier, perhaps *c.*5500BC. At Zohapilco, near the volcano of Tlapacoya to the east of Lake Chalco, settlers had a wide choice of foods: molluscs, turtles and fish from the lake; water lentils and other plants from the marshy shoreline; wild fruits and

deer, rabbits, dogs, coyotes and rodents from the forested hills. The soil was rich and they grew amaranth and early domesticated forms of *teosinte*. Each winter they could also hunt or trap any of a large number of migratory birds such as Canada geese, teals, pintails and mallards. They made tools from locally available andesite and obsidian. However, this attractive setting had its drawback in the form of the nearby volcanoes. Some time before 3000BC, major eruptions devastated the area and people were not able to resettle the lakeside for about 500 years.

COASTAL SETTLEMENTS
At the eastern edge of Mesoamerica, on the Caribbean coast of Belize, groups of people were living in permanent settlements by 4200BC, eating shellfish, fish, turtles, seabirds and reptiles. On the Pacific coast, south of the Sierra Madre del Sur, groups lived at sites near Acapulco in Guerrero and Matanchén in Nayarit. The remains suggest that they lived there at least semi-permanently from as early as 3000BC, eating shrimps, clams and fish. In Veracruz on the coast of the Gulf of Mexico, people lived at Santa Luisa on the Tecolutla river

Above: The countryside of Oaxaca was the setting for an early Mesoamerican cave settlement near Mitla in 7000--5000BC.

in the years 3500–2000BC, by hunting, fishing and gathering wild foods. They left no evidence that they had even begun to experiment with farming. Farther east, beyond the Isthmus of Tehuantepec, the ancestors of the Maya were making a living on the Pacific coasts of Guatemala by *c.*2000BC. People were also settled very early in north-western Yucatán, in the region of the later settlement of Dzibilchaltún, about 20km (12 miles) inland from the coast.

Below: Copper axe heads like these were not made in Mesoamerica before the 9th–10th centuries AD.

URBAN CEREMONIAL CENTRES
c.2500–300BC

In slightly over 2000 years from c.2500 to c.300BC, Mesoamericans laid the foundations of a great civilization. Larger settlements increasingly reliant on farming rather than hunting, gathering and fishing developed. More efficient ways of irrigating and using land meant farmers were able to produce surpluses of food.

Populations rose rapidly and people began to specialize in small industries and crafts, such as producing pottery, tools or items valued for their use in religious ritual. Social divisions emerged and, in some areas, elite groups took control. Public buildings such as temples were raised and large ceremonial centres laid out.

There was busy interaction between population centres, as people shared or swapped products, raw materials, plants and ideas. This enabled the development of a unified Mesoamerican culture and was a precursor of the long-range trade that was later one of the key defining features of Mesoamerica. Stonemasons began to use basic hieroglyphic signs. The first great Mesoamerican culture, that of the Olmec people, emerged about 1500BC in southern Veracruz and grew to a peak between 1100–600BC.

Below: At Izapa on the Pacific coastal plain of south-east Mexico, Maya settlers built a pyramid (Mound 30a) in 800–500BC.

Above: The image of the ruler in a monster's mouth representing the entrance to the spirit world was established by the time of the Olmec.

A major Olmec centre was established at San Lorenzo, at a spot advantageously situated where the Coatzacoalcos and Chiquito rivers meet and close both to lowland forests and resource-rich highlands, overlooking the fertile flood-plain. San Lorenzo was at the height of its power and influence in the years 1150–900BC. Its people established exchange or trading links with sites in Oaxaca, Guerrero and highland Mexico, and Olmec influence spread far and wide.

Between 900 and 700BC, the era of San Lorenzo came to an end: the Olmec monuments were attacked, defaced and buried. However, the centre was not abandoned until 400BC. A second major Olmec centre at La Venta, in Tabasco, was constructed from 1150BC onwards and reached its peak in the years 800–500BC. It grew up in a region where villagers had been living and raising maize since c.2250BC, supplementing their diet with crocodiles, toads and aquatic birds. The Olmec centre at La Venta was a large ceremonial site containing several

platforms and pyramids generally oriented north–south, but set at 8 degrees west of true north – as at San Lorenzo. It also contained carved colossal heads, whose individuality suggests that they might be portrayals of rulers, and other monuments. The main Olmec sites were probably independent of each other. There was certainly no Olmec empire and there is no real evidence of military conquest – although Altar 4 at La Venta and Monument 14 at San Lorenzo bear carvings of one figure leading another by a rope, suggesting a captor and his captive and indicating there were inter-city rivalries.

OAXACAN HIGHLANDS

In the area of the modern Mexican state of Oaxaca, San José Mogote became an important centre. From a few simple public buildings c.1350BC, the settlement grew to cover 20ha (50 acres) by 1000BC, with splendid stone temples and platforms. Its creators were independent of, but influenced by, the Olmec. San José's public buildings, like those at San Lorenzo, were oriented 8 degrees west of north. Craftsmen lived in quarters according to their speciality – for example, tool manufacturers, jade workers and basket-makers lived in separate areas.

Around 500BC the great Zapotec city of Monte Albán was established nearby in a hilltop position dominating the three valleys of Zaachila to the south, Etla to the north and Tlacolula to the east. The hilltop, 400m (1,300ft) above the floor of the valleys, was a strategic position that would have been easily defended in conflict, but there is no archaeological evidence that the city was ever attacked. This inspires historians to argue that the hilltop may simply have been chosen by competing Zapotec valley groups as a neutral setting for a central ceremonial and administrative settlement.

Left: This stone pillar is one of the few pieces of Olmec monumental art to represent a woman. It was found in 1925.

ABOVE THE VALLEY OF MEXICO

The village of Coapexco, perched at an altitude of 2,600m (8,500ft) on the side of Mount Ixtaccíhuatl, appears to have been a centre for trade in the highly prized volcanic glass obsidian c.1200BC, or it was perhaps the home to manufacturers of obsidian blades – archaeologists have found obsidian from distant and exotic sources at the site. Below in the Valley of Mexico villages established at Tlatilco on the western edge of Lake Texcoco and at Tlapacoya on the shore of Lake Chalco left remarkable stores of skilfully hand-modelled ceramic figures dating from c.1100BC. They represent mothers with babies, ball players, dwarfs, musicians, shamans, acrobats, hunchbacks and musicians. Some were found in household waste, but others were placed in graves: as many as 60 were interred in a single grave at Tlatilco.

A ceremonial centre was constructed at Cuicuilco to the west of Lake Xochimilco in the Valley of Mexico c.400BC. Labourers raised a pyramid in four stages, from a circular base, finally facing it in stone and building two staircases climbing 27m (90ft) to a platform that held twin shrines. This is the earliest

Above: Olmec centres existed at Tres Zapotes, Río Chiquito, Portero Nuevo and Laguna de Los Cerros as well as at La Venta and San Lorenzo. Olmec influence spread as far as Chalcatzingo and Guatemala.

known pyramid-platform supporting two shrines. This feature would be adopted by many Mesoamerican peoples including the Aztecs, whose Great Pyramid in Tenochtitlán bore twin shrines to Tláloc and Huitzilopochtli. Cuicuilco rose to become a major population centre covering 400ha (1,000 acres) and home to 20,000 people. Just 1km (0.6 miles) to the east lay a collection of 11 sacred mounds at Peña Pobre.

CENTRAL AND SOUTHERN MAYA

The site of Nakbé in the lowlands of Guatemala was one of the pioneer centres of Maya civilization and was well established by 600BC. Public buildings included temples dedicated to the gods rather than individual rulers.

In southern Maya lands by c. 1800BC, people along the Pacific coast of Guatemala were living in permanent villages of 400–1,000 inhabitants, a size that suggests that a chieftain or leader was in control of the village. He might have established pre-eminence by giving gifts. The people of these settlements began to specialize in making salt, in fishing and in pottery.

THE RISE OF THE GREAT CITIES
300BC–AD250

The 500-odd years from 300BC to AD250 saw the emergence of great cities ruled by a king or members of a powerful elite. In the central highlands of Mexico, the most important was Teotihuacán, in the north-east part of the Valley of Mexico. In Oaxaca, Monte Albán was dominant. In the central Maya region, several significant centres emerged, including El Mirador and Tikal, where large stucco masks carved on temples and pyramids celebrated powerful royal dynasties.

A vibrant trade and exchange network arose and the elite groups clearly possessed great wealth. This is evident from the richness of palaces and other upper-class residences, the construction of lavish tombs and the laying out of wealthy grave offerings. The people of Teotihuacán prospered by trade rather than war, but the other major cities were built with the spoils of conquest. The Zapotecs of Monte Albán made a number of conquests and forced several communities to pay tribute. The cities of the central Maya region waged bitter war. Many centres – including Tikal, Monte Albán, Calakmul and Edzna – erected defensive walls and dug moats. Carved images of the period depict prisoners of war and sacrificial victims.

Above: The Zapotecs of Monte Albán had laid out their ball court on the north-eastern corner of the Great Plaza by AD100.

THE HOLY CITY

At the start of the period, Teotihuacán in the north-east part of the Valley of Mexico began to emerge as a centre to rival Cuicuilco in the southern part of the valley. Villages had existed in the Teotihuacán region since c.900BC.

The area was an ancient religious centre because of its network of caves and tunnels. (Mesoamericans viewed caverns as sacred places providing access to the underworld.) By c.300BC, Teotihuacán was growing, with evidence of obsidian workshops and other craft centres.

Both Cuicuilco and Teotihuacán drew people from throughout the Valley of Mexico; the two centres may have been rivals and perhaps even foes, as fortified and hilltop sites developed around the lakes of the Valley of Mexico in this period. However, an eruption of the Xitle volcano near Cuicuilco c.50 BC decided the matter. The area around Cuicuilco was devastated and the city abandoned in favour of Teotihuacán. The latter expanded rapidly: by AD150, it covered 20km (12 miles) and was home to around 80,000 people. Elsewhere in the Valley of Mexico settlers established villages for the first time on the eastern edge of Lake Texcoco. They could not farm these lands, so must have made their living from the waters of the lake.

OAXACA

In Oaxaca, Monte Albán established itself as the capital of the whole region, powerful in trade. Population rose from around 7,000 in 300BC to as many as 17,000 inhabitants one hundred years later, living in three distinct communities. As the centre of Monte Albán grew in importance and wealth, so did the area's previously pre-eminent community, San José Mogote, gradually become abandoned.

Like the Olmec before, the ruling elite in Monte Albán was able to command a vast labour force. Around the city's western and northern edge, 3km (2 miles) of defensive walls up to 4m (13ft) high were erected in a massive building project.

Left: This pyramid (E-VII) at Uaxactún is part of the Group E sacred complex aligned to solar and astronomical events.

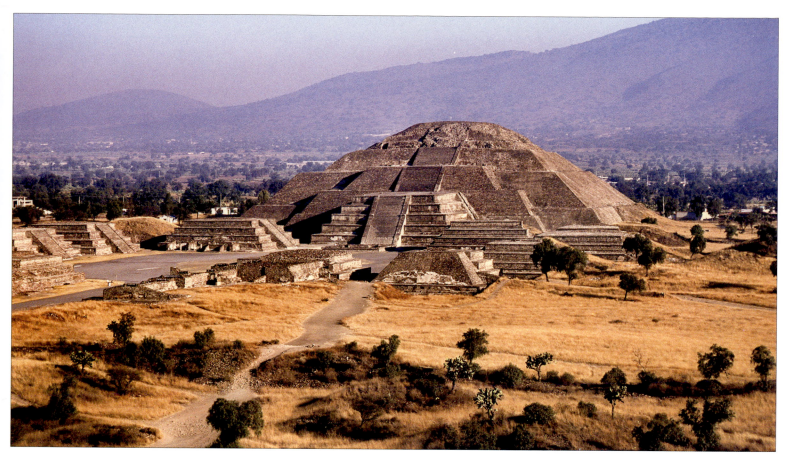

Another Oaxaca people, the Mixtecs, built hilltop centres at Yucuita and Monte Negro at the two ends of the Nochixtlán Valley in this era. Both featured ceremonial buildings laid out on an L plan, rather than around a plaza. Both sites were at their apogee *c.* 200BC.

SOUTHERN AND CENTRAL MAYA
In contrast to the far-reaching centralized powers of Teotihuacán and Monte Albán, in Maya territories several small, competing kingdoms developed.

In the southern Maya region, Kaminaljuyú was established in the Valley of Guatemala. In the years 400BC–AD100 its people laid out a large ritual centre, with several temple-pyramids – some containing burials – on either side of a long rectangular plaza or ceremonial way. Surviving statues depict rulers with divine characteristics – some wear a bird mask. These, together with lavish elite burials, suggest that the Kaminaljuyú nobility ruled with absolute authority. Izapa – on the Pacific coastal plain below the Sierra Madre de Chiapas – underwent a great expansion: more than 250 stone stelae, altars and carved boulders were added in 300–50BC. The style of carving on these

stelae, which reveals some Olmec influence, would become highly influential, spreading as far to the east as the settlements of Belize and as far to the west as Tres Zapotes and Veracruz. Other expanding sites in the Pacific coastal region included Abaj Takalik, El Baúl, Monte Alto and Santa Leticia.

In the central Maya region, El Mirador was the largest city of this era, built *c.*150BC–AD150. It was at the hub of a system of causeways that linked it to several other cities, including Nakbé. Its central area was 2km (1⅕ miles) across and contained the vast El Tigre monument, which consists of a central pyramid with two smaller adjoining structures, all erected on a single base – and has a surface area six times larger than that of Temple IV, the largest building at nearby Tikal. Some historians believe that, alongside the settlement at Calakmul in the Campeche region of Mexico, El Mirador governed a state encompassing 10,000km (6,200 miles); monuments at Calakmul and El Mirador celebrated the same ancestral gods.

Tikal grew from a village in 300BC to a major dynastic city by AD300. Its oldest ceremonial structure, the North

Above: The Pyramid of the Moon, which is 46m (151ft) high, was built in Teotihuacán in the 1st century AD.

Acropolis, was begun *c.*250BC. The Mundo Perdido ('Lost World') complex was rebuilt many times up to AD300. A stela celebrating King Jaguar Paw I (*r.* AD278–317) erected in AD292 is the oldest known stela marked with a date in the Maya Long Count in the lowlands.

At Uaxactún, four temples were laid out according to precise astronomical alignment, in a pattern copied in many other cities, known to archaeologists as Group E. In this arrangement, three temples on the eastern side of a court were aligned so that at solstices and equinoxes the sun would rise above one of them when viewed from a fourth building erected to the west. Using these sightings, priests could keep precise track of time by pinpointing the year's shortest and longest days.

Río Azul in north-east Guatemala was established on the banks of the river Azul. Two temple platforms were built there in this era. In Belize, pyramids and plazas were laid out to celebrate the power of the king of Cerros beginning in 50BC.

35

THE GLORY OF TEOTIHUACÁN
AD300–500

Teotihuacán continued to expand in size and influence. Thousands of apartment buildings were constructed in the years AD300–500. They were built in compounds, each with room for 60–100 people, probably grouped by kin relationship or craft specialization. Elite dwellings alongside the Street of the Dead were built for higher social groups. The city reached its peak c.AD500, with a population of 125,000–200,000. This made it the sixth largest city in the world at the time.

GROWING SPHERE OF INFLUENCE
Some members of this vast population were incomers from other parts of Mesoamerica. One area in the north-eastern part of the city was dubbed the Merchants' Barrio by archaeologists because a large amount of pottery from other Mesoamerican regions was found there. Historians now believe that people from the Gulf coast and the central Maya region made their home there in the years AD300–500. Farther west, another part of the city was home to Zapotec incomers from the Oaxaca region.

Teotihuacán was a major religious centre, built on an ancient sacred site. More than 1,000 shrines and temples lined the Street of the Dead. A large number of full-time priests and temple staff must have resided in the city. Nevertheless, two-thirds of the population were farmers, primarily raising crops of amaranth, maize and squash. Some 9,700 hectares were irrigated, stretching to a distance of around 15km (9 miles) from the city centre. Many artisans and traders lived and worked in the city and its influence – so significant and far-reaching that one could almost speak of an empire – was spread by trade and exchange rather than by war or threat of military force.

The Maya city of Kaminaljuyú in the Guatemala Valley was drawn into Teotihuacán's sphere of influence through trade, probably in obsidian from the

Left: Clay figurines, such as this warrior, were used in religious rites in Teotihuacano homes.

Guatemalan site of El Chayal. In this period, Kaminaljuyú's ceremonial centre was remodelled in the *talud-tablero* (sloping apron/vertical panel) architectural style of Teotihuacán. There might even have been intermarriage between the elites of the two cities. Teotihuacán traders also established a centre at Matacapan in Veracruz in AD400–500.

Monte Albán also continued to thrive, and its population grew. Farmers began to specialize, promoting the growth of a market in agricultural goods. The Zapotecs established a sacred site at Mitla in the Oaxaca region after c.AD300. Its name comes from its Aztec Nahuatl name *Mictlan* ('Realm of the Dead').

CENTRAL MAYA REGION
In the central Maya region, the population reached a maximum of about a million by c.AD300, after 600 years of steady growth since 300BC. Tikal rose to a pre-eminent position, eclipsing the power of El Mirador.

Many buildings in the North Acropolis were built over earlier constructions between AD250 and AD550. The area was a necropolis celebrating the city's ruling dynasty: eight funerary temples were laid out in a symmetrical pattern on a vast platform of 80m (260ft) by 100m (320ft). Like the structures at Kaminaljuyú, Tikal's buildings show evidence of the influence of Teotihuacano *talud-tablero* architectural style.

A ruler named Yax Moch Xoc was afterwards celebrated at Tikal as the founder of this dynasty. He laid the foundations of Tikal's greatness by establishing the city as an independent ruling centre either through political acumen or military might. His early successors included Moon Zero Bird (whose accession c.AD320 and might are celebrated on the jadeite celt known to scholars as the Leyden plaque) and the great king Stormy Sky, whose mortuary shrine was built in Tikal's North Acropolis.

Lowland rivals Tikal and Uaxactún were drawn into increasingly fierce competition that culminated in AD378 when Tikal took control of its rival. A member of the Tikal dynastic elite named Smoking Frog – perhaps the brother of King Great Jaguar Paw – was either installed on the throne at Uaxactún or led a successful war against the city and seized power there. Two carved monuments at each site commemorate the event: bodies found in a tomb at Uaxactún near one of these monuments may be those of the Uaxactún king's family, buried there while the defeated king himself was taken to Tikal for ceremonial slaughter. In the reign of Smoking Frog's successor, Curl Nose, Tikal appears also to have conquered Río Azul c.AD385: altars at Río Azul commemorate the execution of eight local rulers, and Tikal kings are commemorated elsewhere at the site.

Tikal maintained close links to southern Mayan centres, notably Kaminaljuyú. The tomb of the Tikal king Curl Nose, who died c.AD425, contains offerings that prove links with elite burals at Kaminaljuyú. Some scholars have suggested that Curl Nose was a native of Kaminaljuyú who married into the ruling Tikal dynasty. By this route, the influence of Teotihuacán, which was strong at Kaminaljuyú, might have reached Tikal and can be seen in the style of carvings during the reigns of Curl Nose and his son and successor Stormy Sky.

Above: Monte Albán temples use a version of the talud-tablero *(sloping apron/vertical panel) design developed in Teotihuacán.*

Alternatively, there might have been direct trading contacts between Teotihuacán and Tikal. In Stormy Sky's reign, Tikal's power spread further still, to reach Yaxchilán, Quiriguá and even Copán in modern Honduras. A Tikal emblem was carved on a lintel at Yaxchilán c.AD504 and a style associated with Tikal appeared in the carving of monuments at both Copán and Quiriguá during this period.

SOUTHERN MAYA REGION

In the south-east Maya lowlands, Copán in western Honduras became a major centre in the 5th century AD. People had lived in villages in this fertile valley setting since c.1000BC, but the settlement began to expand significantly from c.AD250 onwards. The great dynasty of Copán was founded by Yax Kuk Mo' in AD426. In his reign, the first ritual and administrative buildings were erected at Copán.

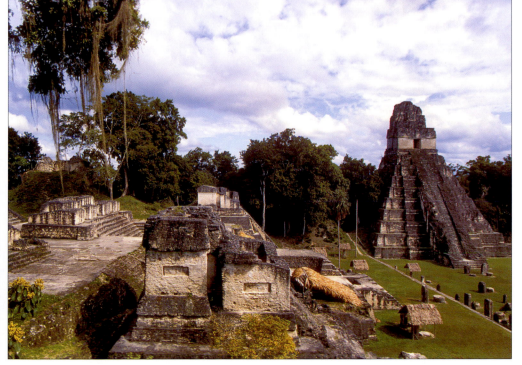

Left: Tikal's North Acropolis is one of the city's oldest parts. The towering Temple I (right) was built in the 8th century AD.

POWER CHANGES HANDS
AD500–700

Teotihuacán continued to thrive until *c.*AD550–650, when its vibrant trading network began to fail in the face of competition from the east. In the period up to *c.*AD750, the city maintained a prosperous appearance, despite the fact that decline had set in. The palace of Quetzalpapálotl in the south-west of the Plaza of the Moon, was built after AD500 and the magnificent murals in the Techinantitla apartment building were painted *c.*AD650–750.

Monte Albán expanded greatly in the years AD500–750, covering 6.5km (4 miles) and supporting a population of as many as 24,000.

There were friendly relations between the Zapotec capital and Teotihuacán. Not only were Zapotecs resident in Teotihuacán but, according to carvings on stelae at the South Platform of the Main Plaza at Monte Albán, Teotihuacáno diplomats paid a state visit to the Oaxacan capital.

Below: The Palace of Quetzalpapálotl is an example of the high-status residential and public buildings that continued to be erected in Teotihuacán, despite the city's continuing decline.

Above: This figurine, found in Palenque, represents one of the members of the city's elite group of astronomer-priests.

CENTRAL MAYA REGION

Population of the Maya lowlands in AD500 was an estimated one million, but by *c.*AD600, numbers of people began to climb very significantly, reaching a peak *c.*AD800 of 2.6–3.4 million.

In the first part of this period Tikal continued to thrive. Its success throughout this early-to-mid Classic Period was derived partly from its position: the site was rich in the highly prized natural resource of flint (needed for making chipped stone tools), and lay close to two seasonal swamps or lakes that could be used for intensive farming. The swamps, situated to east and west, helped to make the site easily defensible in times of conflict. Close to rivers that connected it ultimately both to the Gulf and to the Caribbean, Tikal was ideally situated for trade and commerce.

The city appears to have had a vibrant society, with potential for upward movement through military or trading success and this probably helped to inspire its rise and expansion. Tikal was also a major religious centre and place of pilgrimage. It was, finally, one of the pioneers of dynastic kingship in the Maya world. When places such as Calakmul, Yaxchilán, Caracol and Copán were rising to prominence, Tikal was revered as a divinely inspired forerunner.

However, from *c.*AD530, Tikal's position was eclipsed by rivals for a period and its wealth declined severely for about 150 years. Following an attack on Caracol in AD556, in the reign of the Tikal king Double Bird, Tikal was defeated by its rival. A carved ball game marker at Caracol, which archaeologists used to believe was an altar and therefore labelled Altar 21, celebrates the victory of King Lord Water over Tikal in AD562. This probably led to the sacrifice of Double Bird. Tikal entered a period in which its royal burials were far less rich and no significant stelae were erected. The city might well have been diverting much of

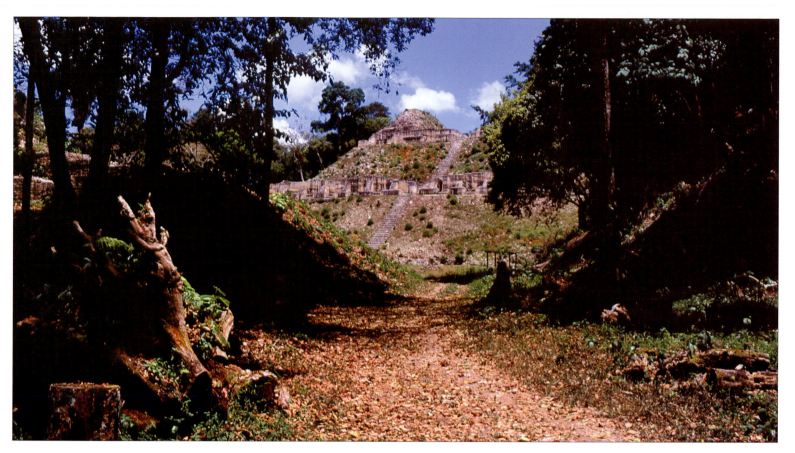

Above: Caracol was a major Maya city in Belize. Its core contained 128 plaza groups; the site covered 50sq km (19sq miles).

its wealth to Caracol, which expanded greatly, and Tikal's rulers may have been forbidden by Caracol to erect any stelae.

Refugees from Tikal travelled southwards to the rainforested Petexbatun region close to a major tributary of the Usumacinta river named the Pasión river, where they founded twin capitals at Dos Pilas and Aguateca. The first ruler, Flint Sky, was in power in Dos Pilas in AD647. His emblem glyph was almost identical to that of the Tikal dynasty. Meanwhile, Calakmul in the south-eastern Campeche region of Mexico rose to prominence in the years after AD600 and was an ally of Caracol in wars in the Maya lowlands. With Calakmul's backing, Caracol defeated Naranjo in AD631. Calakmul also entered into alliance with Dos Pilas.

Dos Pilas went on to challenge the formerly mighty Tikal and fought several campaigns, culminating in the defeat of the Tikal ruler Shield Skull by Flint Sky of Dos Pilas in AD679. Flint Sky celebrated his victories in a hieroglyphic stairway at Dos Pilas. However, Tikal's pride was to be reborn. In AD695, King

Ah Cacau of Tikal captured and sacrificed Jaguar Paw-Jaguar of Calakmul. Meanwhile, in the south-western Maya lowlands, Palenque established itself as a major power and the dominant force in the region in the early 7th century AD. Inscriptions at the site provide a long dynastic list, going back as far as the probable founder, Balam Kuk, who came to the throne in AD431 and even further beyond to an assuredly mythical figure named Kin Chan, who was said to have come to the throne in 967BC. However, the city's great success coincided with the long and stable reign of King Pacal, whose splendid tomb would be laid beneath the Temple of Inscriptions in his city. Pacal came to the throne in AD615 and the earliest surviving use of the Palenque emblem glyph is dated to his reign.

SOUTHERN MAYA REGION

Kaminaljuyú thrived greatly by trade in obsidian, but began to decline after AD550, perhaps because the waning of Teotihuacán affected trade. The settlements of the Guatemala Valley became markedly less prosperous and were abandoned altogether by c.AD800, as their inhabitants retreated to more easily fortified and defended hilltop positions.

Copán greatly expanded its sphere of influence, particularly in the long reigns of Butz' Chan (AD578–628) and Smoke Jaguar (AD628–95). In this time of great dynastic strength and stability, Copán took control of Quiriguá in AD653 and of much of the valley of the Motagua river, and thus of the trade in jade and obsidian that travelled down that corridor from the highlands to the Caribbean sea.

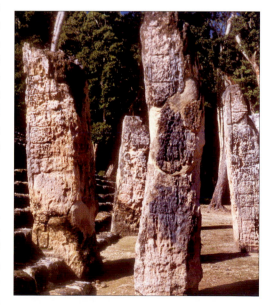

Above: Stelae celebrate rulers of Calakmul in south-eastern Campeche. Calakmul was at least as large as its famed rival Tikal.

39

THE COLLAPSE OF SOCIAL ORDER
AD700–900

In the years after AD700, Teotihuacán continued its slow collapse in prestige and power as the city's merchants endured the decay of the trade network that had once connected them to Veracruz, Tikal, the Guatemala Valley and beyond. After a fire c.AD750, the centre was abandoned, but about 40,000 people continued to live in outlying parts of the city. Monte Albán declined at the same time, beginning c.AD750, as the people of the Oaxaca valleys turned to local centres such as Lambityeco and Jalieza rather than the regional capital for the focus of their ritual life and work. Monte Albán's hilltop was abandoned and its population declined to about 4,000 by AD900.

The collapse of the centuries-old social order embodied by large centres such as Teotihuacán created a period of flux and of military conflict between small kingdoms. Peoples competed for trade and pre-eminence: many groups were on the move in the 7th, 8th and 9th centuries, leading to shifts in balance of

Below: Xochicalco and El Tajín were among the centres that rose to prominence with the decline of Teotihuacán and Monte Albán.

power and the emergence of new settlements. A Maya group named the Olmeca-Xicalanga travelled westwards from southern Veracruz and Tabasco to establish their capital in the fortress of Cacaxtla, on a hilltop dominating the Tlaxcala Valley, some time after AD650. The city, renowned for its murals, was at its peak until AD900. Settlements were established at Azcopatzalco, Cerro Portesuelo, Xico and Cerro de la Estrella in the Valley of Mexico.

To the south of the Valley of Mexico the fortified city of Xochicalco, in the western part of the Morelos region, won itself a regional state reaching west into the Balsas Depression, north into the Ajusco Mountains and south-west into the region known as Mixteca Baja. Xochicalco, although occupied in the previous centuries, was at its height in the years c.AD700–900.

In the tropical rainforest of northern Veracruz, El Tajín became an important centre. The site had been settled as early as c.AD100 and had thrived by contact with Teotihuacán: as Teotihuacáno influence waned, El Tajín began to assert its authority over its region. The same

Above: Carved columns on the roof of the Temple of the Warriors, Chichén Itzá, once supported the roof. The Castillo is beyond.

process – of increasing independence following the decline of Teotihuacán – applied to Cholula (in modern Puebla) and other city-states.

THE RISE OF THE ITZÁ

Other Maya groups known as the Chontal-speaking Maya, the Putún and the Itzá spread out from a base in the region of Chontalapa, in northern coastal Tabasco and south-western Campeche, at the western edge of the Yucatán peninsula. They were warrior-merchants, seeking political control and wealth through trade. Some established themselves at Palenque in the 7th to 9th centuries, others moved inland along the Usumacinta river to Yaxchilán, Altar de Sacrificios and Seibal. Putún Maya may have travelled into the southern Maya region along the upper reaches of the Usumacinta in the northern highlands.

The Itzá moved up the western coast of the Yucatán peninsula, then went inland towards the cities of Uxmal and Chichén Itzá. Most historians believe that the Itzá were established in Chichén Itzá by AD850. Inscriptions on important buildings at Chichén Itzá raised in the years AD869–81 praise an early Itzá leader named Kakupacal, who claimed to be related to the dynasty of Palenque.

La Quemada
San Luis Potosí • Panuco
Gulf of Mexico
Dzibilchaltún
Aké
Mérida • • Yaxuna
Tula/Tollán • • El Tajín
Uxmal • Chacchob • Tulúm
Teotihuacán
Veracruz
Edzná • Hochob
Tingambato • Cholula
CAMPECHE Santa Rita
Xochicalco Matacapán • Potonchán • Xicalango Becán •
Comalcalco • Calakmul • Cuelló • Colha
Xochipala Palenque • Tikal • San José
Chilpancingo Toniná • • Holmul
Chiapa • Yaxchilán
Monte Albán de Corzo Bonampak • Seibal
Acapulco • Chama • Pusilha
Tehuantepec Tonalá • Nebaj • Quiriguá
Izapa • Copán •
PACIFIC Kaminaljuyú •
Cotzumalhuapa • Balberta
OCEAN Quelepa •

🔴 Teotihuacano influence
🟣 Maya region
🟡 Zapotec influence

CENTRAL MAYA REGION

In the Petexbatun region, Dos Pilas built a short-lived empire through warfare and diplomacy. After the death of the city's founder, Flint Sky, his son – known to historians as Shield God K – took power in AD698 and entered an alliance with Naranjo. His successor, who is known only as Ruler 3, defeated Seibal in AD735, made a marriage alliance with Cancuén and was also allied to the great power of Caracol. His successor, Ruler 4, extended the empire to cover *c.*4,000km (2,500 miles), but in AD761 he was captured and beheaded by a rival lord at Tamarindito. The power at the centre was gone and the area plunged into bitter conflict. Dos Pilas was largely abandoned after the AD761 war.

Palenque was at war with the city of Toniná in the Ocosingo Valley in the early 8th century. King Kan Xul II of Palenque was captured and beheaded by the ruler of Toniná in AD711.

In the Maya lowlands, Tikal enjoyed a great renaissance after more than 150 years in which it had erected no stelae and apparently suffered a severe decline in wealth. King Ah Cacau restored the city's military and political standing abroad by defeating the rival city of Calakmul and embarked on major building projects at home, including the erection of Temples I and II.

THE MAYA COLLAPSE

In the late 8th and 9th centuries the city-states of the Maya lowlands one by one stopped erecting stelae celebrating their divine kings. The cities fell into decline before being finally abandoned altogether. Historians believe that the decline was caused by a chain of events kick-started by overpopulation in the region, which led to ever more intensive farming and the degradation of the environment, matched by a fiercer form of warfare that focused less on raiding for prestige and more on territorial expansion. The result was population decline – numbers in the southern lowlands fell by one-third in the century after AD830. Several sites – including Piedras Negras, Quiriguá, Naranjo and Calakmul – erected their last stela in AD810. The last carved stela was raised at Caracol in AD859 and at Tikal in AD869.

At Tikal, as at Dos Pilas and many other formerly magnificent centres, the cities were invaded by squatters who eked out a living in thatched homes on the great ceremonial plazas: they were not afraid to move monuments and even break into the tombs of once great kings in search of riches. However, this collapse

Above: A Cacaxtla mural figure showing a man transformed into a jaguar, c.AD900.

did not take effect farther east in coastal or riverside settlements in Belize, where Rita Caracol, Lamanai and other sites continued to thrive after AD900.

Quiriguá in the Motagua Valley had been subject to Copán since AD653, but rose to challenge its overlord. In AD738 Cauac Sky of Quiriguá beheaded King 18 Rabbit of Copán. In this way, Quiriguá gained control of the lucrative trade in obsidian, jade and other items passing from the Guatemalan highlands along the Motagua valley.

THE TRIUMPH OF THE TOLTECS
AD900–1200

The city of Tollán (modern Tula) in the state of Hidalgo took over from Teotihuacán as the pre-eminent centre of highland Mexico c.AD950. It stood on a ridge overlooking a tributary of the Pánuco river named the Tula, near to the northern limit of Mesoamerica. It ruled for more than 200 years.

HOME OF THE TOLTECS
The Aztecs and early chroniclers wove a web of religious narrative around the origins of this city, home to the Toltecs so revered by the Méxica of Tenochtitlán and also to the great feathered serpent god, Quetzalcóatl. According to this narrative, Quetzalcóatl or Ce Acatl Topiltzin was the son of a leader of the Chichimec people, who left his home at

Above: Each of the temple-top figures at Tollán (Tula) wears warrior garb: a butterfly breastplate and feathered headdress.

Culhuacán in the Valley of Mexico to assume leadership of the Toltec community of Tollán. Here he presided over a wondrous age of artistic expression and scientific achievement, but a Toltec named Huastec – in conjunction with Tezcatlipoca, god of darkness and fate – brought disgrace upon Ce Acatl Topiltzin, who departed from the city. Different versions recount that he either cast himself on a sacrificial pyre and rose into the heavens as the planet Venus or that he sailed away to the east on a raft of snakes, promising to return.

Historians do not know for sure who the Toltec founders of Tollán were. The evidence suggests that they were warlike incomers from the north.

The city they built covered 13sq km (8sq miles) and was home to a population of up to 60,000 people. It was a centre for craftspeople working obsidian, making pots, stoneware and tools from chert. The ritual centre – consisting of two plazas, two pyramids, meeting halls and two ball courts – was oriented precisely 18 degrees east of true north.

From Tollán the Toltecs exerted control over – and probably received tribute from – a sizeable area, incorporating the northern part of the Valley of Mexico, the region of modern Hidalgo state as far east as Tulancingo, plus the Toluca Valley, areas of the Bajío and territories around the Lerma River. The empire's days of glory were numbered, however, and the city was overrun and burned c.1150–1200.

In the period of Tollán's pre-eminence, the settlement of Cholula in the Puebla region of Mexico was also thriving. The town's wealth and prestige were such that its pyramid was rebuilt to a height of 55m (180ft). Historians are uncertain whether Cholula was a rival or an ally of Tollán.

CHICHÉN ITZÁ
Another legend concerning the Toltecs suggests that a group from Tollán led by Quetzalcóatl travelled to the Gulf Coast in the 10th century and then under the

Below: Towering carved warriors facing west atop the Temple of Tlahuizcalpantecuhtli at Tollán (Tula) proclaim Toltec might.

Above: The six tiers and crowning temple of the Pyramid of the Niches, El Tajín, were built over a similar earlier version of the building.

leadership of Kukulcán (the Maya form of Quetzalcóatl) made their way to northern Yucatán, where they settled in Chichén Itzá. Many elements of Toltec/Mexican style in architecture and religious iconography appeared at Chichén Itzá; these were most likely spread through trade.

Chichén Itzá was by now the heart of a growing tributary empire. The Tutil Xiu, an Itzá elite and ruling dynasty, grew wealthy by trading in salt from the Yucatán salt beds, in obsidian, which they imported from Mexico, in ceramics and in basalt. They developed port facilities on Ilsa Cerritos, an island just off the northern coast of Yucatán. They ruled through a group of nobles rather than

through a single, divinely blessed king. However, the Itzá apparently made many enemies, for native chronicles contain many slighting references to these successful incomers. Around 1100, the city of Mayapán was founded around 100km (80 miles) to the west of Chichén Itzá and quickly became its principal rival.

A NICHE IN VERACRUZ

El Tajín continued to thrive in northern Veracruz. Its six-tier Pyramid of the Niches is an elaborate variation on Teotihuacáno *talud-tablero* architectural style. The site also contains no fewer than 12 ball courts: the city may have been a centre for playing the game and could have hosted regional competitions. There is even the possibility that many centuries before El Tajín's independent glory, the ball game could have been developed in this part of Mesoamerica.

SOUTHERN MAYA LANDS

In the period of Chichén Itzá's glory, northern raiders appear to have brought terror to Southern Maya regions, where many settlements on valley floors were abandoned as people moved to easily defensible hilltop settings, and built ditches, walls and other fortifications. These incomers came either from northern Yucatán or from the Gulf Coast region of Chontalapa. They brought their architectural style and warrior imagery along with them.

A settlement at Chuitinamit-Atitlan on Lake Atitlan has a carving of a feathered serpent mouth opening to release human heads that is reminiscent of imagery at Chichén Itzá. Another at Chalchitan, on the Uscaminta tributary the Chixoy, contains a platform that may be a Chichén Itzá-style skull rack or *tzompantli*, on which skulls were displayed.

LAND RAIDERS
1200–1325

Tollán was sacked by raiders in *c*.1150–1200. The city's violent demise was followed by 150 years of turmoil in the central highlands of Mexico, as warring groups of nomads known collectively as Chichimecs ('Sons of the Dog') spread through the Valley of Mexico and beyond, scrambling for control of the strategic settlements and well-watered agricultural land. All claimed descent from the Toltecs and a link to the glory that had been Tollán.

RICH PICKINGS
One powerful Chichimec leader, Xólotl, founded the settlement of Tenayuca, to the west of Lake Texcoco, then later transferred his capital across the water to establish Texcoco. Another group, which claimed to have the closest links to the Toltecs, settled at Culhuacán, south of the lake. The Tepanecs settled at Azcapotzalco, which had been founded towards the end of Teotihuacán's era of

Below: The fortress-town of Tulum, above the Caribbean Sea, was protected by cliffs and an 800m (half-mile) wall.

glory *c*.AD800–900. Lands all around Lake Texcoco were settled by Chichimecs and descendants of survivors from the fall of Teotihuacán and Tollán: towards the northern end were Tenayuca and Azcapotzalco; to the east lay Huextola and Coatlichan; to the south was Chalco, Cuitláhauc, Xochimilco, Xico, Mixquic

Above: Five circular platforms supported temples and might have housed elite burials in the Tarascan capital, Tzintzuntzan.

and Amecameca as well as Culhuacán. A tribe calling themselves the México, who were destined to establish the Aztec empire, came into the region after all the best land had been taken, probably towards the end of the 13th century.

THE FIRST AZTECS
Historians cannot easily supply an accurate account of the early years of the tribe, for the México/Aztecs later embellished their history in an attempt to justify their standing and to emphasize their links to the Toltecs of yore. It appears that they came into the region under the leadership of Tenoch, and settled near Chapultepec to the west of Lake Texcoco. When they were attacked by the Tepanecs of Azcapotzalco and the people of Culhuacán, the México cast themselves upon the mercy of Culhuacán. They settled nearby at a place named Tizapán and proved themselves capable agriculturists, adapting swiftly to the lakeside setting. They married into local families

and began to call themselves the Méxica-Culhua. They fought alongside the Culhua against Xochimilco and also served the Tepanecs of Azcapotzalco. Then, after a dramatic dispute with the leaders of Culhuacán – in one account after they sacrificed the daughter of a leading Culhua lord – they moved on to the south and established their own city, named Tenochtitlán in Tenoch's honour, on an island in Lake Texcoco. This probably occurred in 1325. Tenoch was the first leader of Tenochtitlán, and was celebrated as *tlatoani* ('He who Speaks'), the title given to the ruler of the city, until the collapse of the Aztec empire in 1521.

POWER STRUGGLE IN YUCATÁN

The Tutul Xiu rulers of Chichén Itzá were driven from power in the 13th century by the Cocoms, a rival group of Itzá from Mayapán. According to the chronicles, the Cocoms hired a mercenary named Hunac Ceel from Tabasco who, by trickery and military force, forced the

Below: This haunting shell carving was made by a craftsman from Mayapán, rising power and controller of coastal trade.

Tutul Xiu from power and seized control of the city. The chronicles set these events c.1221 or 1283. There is archaeological evidence that Chichén Itzá was sacked in the early 13th century, but there are also signs that it was gradually abandoned. The Tutul Xiu might have been unable to maintain the elite that gathered around them and the city may also have suffered from drought and starvation.

Whether gradually or at a stroke, Mayapán became the major city of the area and took control of the lucrative coastal trade. It founded a league of city-states in northern Yucatán – itself, Chichén Itzá and Uxmal – that built a tributary empire. In the new capital at Mayapán, the Cocom built a smaller-scale version of the magnificent Temple of Kukulcán at Chichén Itzá. Mayapán was a city of around 15,000 people at its height. As a way of maintaining central authority, the Cocom rulers brought in the heads of tributary-paying states to reside in the capital city, as the Aztecs would later do.

On the east coast of Yucatán the fortified clifftop settlement at Tulum was established c.1200, probably by the rulers of Mayapán, as a coastal trading centre. At Tulum, and nearby Xelhá and Tancah, on the Isla de Cozumel, and farther south on the east coast of Yucatán, several settlements grew prosperous under the rule of the Mayapán alliance.

Above: Mayapán's principal sacred building is the nine-tiered Temple of the Feathered Serpent, now called Kukulcán's Castle.

Some of the survivors of the fall of Chichén Itzá headed south into the rain forests of El Petén and founded a new capital called Tayasal on Lake Petén Itzá in north-western Guatemala. There they would thrive until 1697, when they were finally conquered by the Spanish.

HIGHLAND KINGDOMS

In southern Maya lands, another wave of 'Mexicanized' Putún Maya warriors established kingdoms in the highlands. They arrived from the Gulf Coast lowlands c.1200 and set up mountain-top fortresses from which they brutally subjugated the local people. By c.1350, one group, the Quiché, had established rule over the central highlands. They established their capital, Ismachi, on a narrow piece of land between two ravines.

THE TARASCANS AND TZINTZUNTZAN

At Lake Patzcuaro in Michoacán four communities were established by c.1200: Tzintzuntzan, Ihuatzio, Pátzcuaro and the island settlement of Pacanda. The king of Tzintzuntzan, Tariácuri, took control of the four local powers and set out to forge an empire. This Tarascan kingdom became an arch rival of the Méxica/Aztecs.

THE MÉXICA FORGE AN EMPIRE
1325–1517

On Lake Texcoco, the México/Aztecs founded a second settlement, named Tlatelolco, on a nearby island in 1358. They won acclaim as mercenaries, fighting for Tezozómoc, the Tepanec leader of Azcapotzalco, in wars against Texcoco and Culhuacán, as he built up a great empire.

The México/Aztecs expanded their territorial holdings by gaining *chinampa* agricultural fields in the region of Lake Xochimilco, to the south of Lake Texcoco. However, they came increasingly to resent their subject position and the Tepanecs warily watched their neighbours straining at the leash.

Below: The Selden Codex, *probably written in the Nochixtlán valley, Oaxaca, contains Mixtec genealogies covering AD794–1556.*

In 1428, following the death of Tezozómoc, the México/Aztecs rose up in alliance with Texcoco and Tlacopán to defeat the might of Azcapotzalco. The victorious members of this Triple Alliance divided the Tepanec empire three ways. Tenochtitlán took land to the north and south of Lake Texcoco. Land to the east went to Texcoco and territories in the western part of the Valley of Mexico went to Tlacopán. The Triple Alliance held sway over the Valley of Mexico and beyond until the arrival of the Spanish in the early 16th century. It was the basis of the Aztec empire.

The Aztec *tlatoani* Moctezuma I (*r.* 1440–69) led a great campaign of expansion, extending territorial holdings as far as the Gulf Coast. His successor and

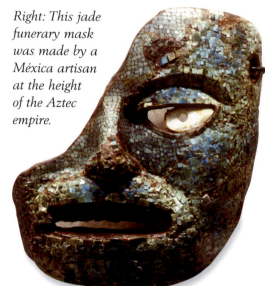

Right: This jade funerary mask was made by a México artisan at the height of the Aztec empire.

grandson Axayácatl (*r.* 1469–81) led campaigns towards the west but was defeated by the Tarascans of Tzintzuntzan, and towards the east where he established control in central parts of Veracruz. He also took control of neighbouring Tlatelolco for Tenochtitlán in 1473. After Axayácatl was succeeded briefly by his undistinguished brother, Tízoc (*r.* 1481–6), a third of Moctezuma's grandsons, Ahuítzotl (*r.* 1486–1502), took power. He gained control over the basin of the Balsas river and coastal lands in Guerrero, as well as much of the Isthmus of Tehauntepec. After several attempts, the Aztecs conquered the sacred site of Mitla, in the Oaxaca region in 1494, and forced the Mixtec residents to pay tribute to Tenochtitlán. Under Moctezuma II in 1519, Aztec imperial holdings covered 150,000sq km (58,000sq miles).

POWER SHIFT IN YUCATÁN
Mayapán was sacked and burned *c.*1450. The nobles of the Tutul Xiu dynasty ousted at Chichén Itzá in the early 13th century had been living in exile among the ruins of Uxmal, a site sacred to them. One of their number, Ah Xupán, led a rebellion against Mayapán's ruling Cocom elite, slaughtering all of the city's rulers bar one, who was on a trading mission.

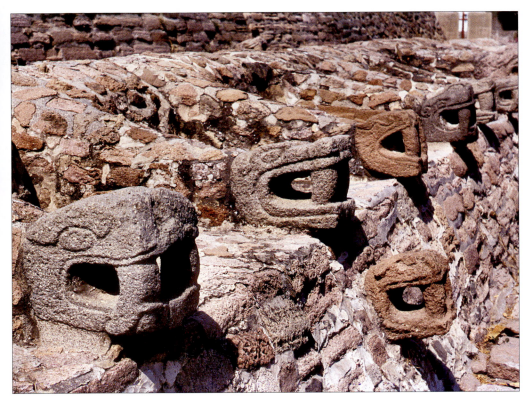

Above: A coatepantli ('serpent wall') encloses three sides of the Aztec pyramid at Tenayuca, near modern Tlalnepantla in Mexico City.

Most of the larger cities of northern Yucatán entered a decline following the fall of Mayapán. Survivors established new cities: one noble family, the Chels, founded Tecoh; the one surviving Cocom ruler made a new start at Tibolon, close to Sotuta. And the Tutul Xiu, glorying in revenge, founded a new settlement at Mani.

In this period, Chichén Itzá and Uxmal were pilgrimage sites, often visited as shrines. Times were hard in northern Yucatán. A hurricane struck in 1464 and the people were severely reduced by a plague in 1480. This was followed by an epidemic of smallpox in 1514.

In the wake of Mayapán's collapse, a settlement was founded at Santa Rita Corozal on the eastern coast at Chetumal Bay. Known as Chetumal, the city was the capital of a state of the same name. Chetumal/Santa Rita Corozal and other settlements in coastal regions of eastern Yucatán continued to thrive until the arrival of the Spanish in the 16th century.

At Tulum and Santa Rita Corozal, delicately rendered murals were painted in the second half of the 15th century in the Mixteca-Puebla style familiar from centres in Puebla and Oaxaca, such as Mitla. A wealthy elite in eastern Yucatán was rich enough to be able to pay for renowned artists from Mexico to produce these splendid wall paintings.

SOUTHERN MAYA LANDS

The Quiché abandoned their capital of Ismachi and founded another, Gumarcaaj or Utatlan, in the early 1400s. They subjugated other peoples and established a Quiché realm, but in 1470 one of these peoples, the Cakchiquels, rebelled and created a rival state. They set up their own capital at Iximche. The two groups fought fiercely. The Cakchiquels held the ascendancy when the Spanish arrived in the region. Other highland city-states included one established by the Pokomam, with a capital at Mixco Viejo; one built by the Mam, with a stronghold at Zaculeu; and the territory of the Tzutuhil at Atitlan, on Lake Atitlan. All these peoples claimed to be descended from the Toltecs.

WESTERN MEXICO

In Michoacán, the small empire of the Tarascans, based at Tzintzuntzan on Lake Pátzcuaro, was strong. They succeeded in holding the Aztecs at bay. Neither the efforts of Moctezuma I nor the expansionist campaigns of Itzcóatl succeeded in bringing the Tarascans into the Aztec empire. The Tarascan army maintained tight control over a small area in the basin of Lake Pátzcuaro within the boundaries of the modern state of Michoacán.

Below: The Mixtecs, Zapotecs, Totonacs and Huastecs were within the Aztec empire, but the Tarascans held imperial forces at bay.

CHAPTER THREE

INFINITE RICHES

All principal Aztec towns in the Valley of Mexico contained a bustling marketplace, located close to the main temple. Merchants were required by law to take their goods to this commercial centre and were forbidden to attempt to sell elsewhere – buyers and sellers risked incurring the wrath of the market god if they did business away from the official place of commerce. On a busy day, 60,000 people might be crammed in the Aztec empire's marketplace in Tlatelolco, Tenochtitlán's twin settlement in Lake Texcoco – making it the largest market in the world at the time. The Aztecs relied on trade – and on goods from an extensive network of tribute-paying areas within the empire – to provide them with foodstuffs, military equipment and other necessaries and with the rare and exotic goods used in their colourful religious ceremonies.

Long-distance trade was a key element of Mesoamerican life, with beginnings in the Olmec civilization of the 2nd millennium BC. Throughout the region's history, trade links between far-flung communities provided conduits along which religious practices, political ideas and artistic styles could pass. Trade was an alternative to warfare as a means of spreading dynastic and political influence, so much so that it is often difficult to establish whether architectural features or religious imagery from the city of Teotihuacán, for example, reached Guatemalan sites such as Kaminaljuyú and Tikal through conquest or trade.

Left: These columns, carved in the Toltec style, stand in the area of Chichén Itzá believed to have been the marketplace.

FIRST TRADERS

Trade flourished in Mesoamerica from early times because of the region's great geographic diversity across relatively short distances. The wide variety of terrain, soil and climate – from tropical jungle to river valley, coastal estuary to highland lake – meant that materials could be found and items manufactured in one setting that were much in demand in a nearby region. Trade networks were established by at least the 2nd millennium BC; they might have grown from a pattern of exchange and gift-giving between elite groups at different sites.

FIRST SETTLEMENTS

The first large Mesoamerican settlements arose in the Gulf Coast lowlands because the productive coastal land allowed its Olmec settlers to produce agricultural surpluses. Elite groups emerged with the power and resources to construct ceremonial and ritual centres. They were also well situated to import raw materials from highland areas inland. At San Lorenzo, on a plateau raised around 50m (164ft) above the surrounding land, settlers built a ritual centre after c.1250BC.

Below: Trade promoted political contact. This Olmec carving from La Venta is thought to be of a visiting ambassador.

Using earth and coloured clay, labourers erected platform mounds around rectangular courts arranged on a north–south axis, but oriented 8 degrees west of true north. They arranged colossal carved stone heads and altars or thrones in the ritual centre.

The basalt for these sculptures was imported from the Tuxtla mountains 70km (40 miles) away; the blocks were carved at the mountains and then floated on rafts by sea and up the Coatzacoalco river to San Lorenzo. Historians believe that the heads were images of Olmec rulers and the large 'altars' were their thrones. A remarkable buried basalt drain was 170m (550ft) long and with three branches, connected to fountains and ponds, which might have been used either functionally or in religious ceremony.

TRADING NETWORKS

The Olmec established centres – such as Chalcatzingo in the valley of the Amatzinac and Teopantecuanitlán rivers close to the Amacuzac river – to trade with and exploit the resources of less developed local cultures. Olmec trading networks extended over very long distances – there is evidence of contact with the valley of the Motagua river in Guatemala and as far as Chalchuapa in El Salvador. The networks distributed goods manufactured in the large Olmec centres in return for minerals and rare stones. In this period the Olmec were probably importing obsidian from or through the village of Coapexco. This clung to the side of the Ixtaccíhuatl

Left: Demand for elite goods propelled the growth of trade. This mask of c.AD200 is made of precious jade.

volcano at a height of 2,600m (8,500ft) and seems to have been a centre for trading in or manufacturing blades of obsidian. Archaeologists have found Olmec pots, grinding tools, ritual figurines and stamps at the site, but they cannot be sure whether these finds are evidence of Olmec trade with local people or of communities of Olmec living in Coapexco.

At Tlatilco on the western shore of Lake Texcoco, people buried their dead with Olmec pots and clay figurines. Here and elsewhere in Oaxaca and Puebla large numbers of Olmec 'dolls' – small hollow clay figures with chubby, outspread legs and baby faces – were collected. Las Bocas in Puebla has yielded a number of these baby figurines and it must have had significant contact with Olmec traders.

TRADING CENTRES

In the Morelos region, Chalcatzingo grew wealthy as a trading centre. The village lies in the valley of the River Amatzinac at the foot of a cliff and would have been well situated as a centre for three trade routes: one heading north to the Valley of Mexico, one going south towards Guerrero and a third running south-east to the Olmec region of the Gulf Coast and the Zapotec sites of Oaxaca. From the Amatzinac valley came cotton, hematite, lime and kaolin; from the region of the Valley of Mexico traders arrived carrying salt and obsidian; while from

Above: Zapotec artists painted this mural in Tomb 105, one of the best-preserved tombs in Monte Albán, c.AD200.

Guerrero merchants came bearing loads of hematite, jadeite and magnetite. Before 1100BC, Chalcatzingo was equipped with a stone-paved public area and two stone-covered platforms about 2m (7ft) in height. Olmec-style monuments were carved in the period 1100–700BC. One, called El Rey by archaeologists, depicts a king or ruler seated in the mouth of a monster that experts identify as the entrance to the underworld; above him are carved rain clouds and three descending raindrops identified as a symbol of authority. This image presents the king as the link between the underworld and the heavens of the rain clouds, like the cosmic tree or world axis. In his person he ensured fertility (rain) and order.

In 700–500BC, Chalcatzingo rose to its highest point of prestige. Many monuments were carved in the style of the Olmec centre at La Venta, which was also then at its peak. The elite rulers of Chalcatzingo, who may have been merchants themselves,

established trading contact with La Venta and elsewhere on the Gulf Coast, with Monte Albán and other Oaxacan sites and with Izapa, far away on the Pacific coastal plain of south-east Mexico.

Another major trading centre of the Olmec era lay in the Guerrero region at Teopantecuanitlán. The site was linked to Chalcatzingo by the Cuautla and Amacuzac rivers, and itself provided

access to the great Balsas river, which could carry loads all the way to the Pacific Ocean. Trading in precious stones, tin, copper and highly prized jade from Guerrero, Teopantecuanitlán became a major centre by 600BC. A pyramid and two ball courts were built and finds of marine shells there suggest that the town was linked to marine trading networks.

In Oaxaca, San José Mogote and other developing villages were trading with San Lorenzo from c.1150BC onwards. Two main lineages or family groups grew prominent, both associated with Olmec motifs. One was linked to the image of the jaguar-faced human or were-jaguar, thought by scholars to represent the earth, while the second was connected to a fire-serpent image thought to be the sign for lightning.

San José Mogote became a great craft centre, with craftsmen housed in one of the four quarters of the settlement according to their speciality.

Left: Spring god Xipe Totec, represented in this Zapotec brazier, may have derived from an Olmec deity known as God VI.

A CITY OF MERCHANTS

The great city of Teotihuacán was a beacon for merchants. It was a major centre for Mesoamerican trade in obsidian, the volcanic glass. This was in demand because craftsmen could fashion it into mirrors, dart-tips for weapons and cutting edges used both in everyday activities and in sacred ritual for letting blood and dispatching sacrificial victims.

Teotihuacán grew up on an ancient site of pilgrimage, and could support a rising population because its position on the San Juan Teotihuacán river made irrigation of farm fields easy. It thrived because it was close to sources of obsidian and because it lay on a major trade route running from the Valley of Mexico to the Gulf Coast.

OBSIDIAN AND OTHER GOODS

In the city's workshops, workers manufactured stone masks, ceremonial tripod vessels, obsidian blades, household furnishings, clay figurines, stone and basalt tools, stonework in shell, serpentine and jade, domestic pots and ornaments of slate. Merchants sold a range of manufactured goods to the large population or organized their export far and wide. Teotihuacáno interests also controlled a

Below: Teotihuacán was renowned from ancient times as a sacred site as well as a major trade centre.

Right: Quetzalcóatl's head adorns the staircase of the Temple of Quetzalcóatl at Teotihuacán.

major obsidian-processing site at Tepeapulco, to the north-east of the city. Obsidian forms when igneous volcanic flow cools rapidly and is only found in highland areas with active volcanoes. The glass appears black, but when some varieties are fashioned into flakes or a transparent edge, the colours grey and green are visible. Minerals in the molten matrix can also produce green obsidian, and because this form was much rarer in Mesoamerica than black-grey obsidian it was consequently much more highly valued. Near Teotihuacán, there was only one source of green obsidian, Cerro de las Navajas at Puchuca, in modern Hidalgo state, but there were at least 15 sources of black and grey obsidian.

By performing trace-element analysis, geochemists have established the source of the obsidian worked in or around Teotihuacán. In workshops at Tepeapulco, workers manufactured items from obsidian which were delivered by footpath from sources at Cerro de las Navajas, at Tulancingo, Paredón and Barrance de los Estetes. From here blades, darts, sacrificial knives and other artefacts were transported to Tulancingo in the Metztitlán Valley and from there to sites such as El Tajín.

Tepeapulco was the centre of Teotihuacán's obsidian industry, but there were also obsidian craftsmen within the city. One group near the Great Compound, for example, specialized in working high-status green obsidian.

Teotihuacán also controlled trade in and distribution of fine-paste pottery bowls and effigy jars known to archaeologists as thin orange pottery. As many as eight settlements in the region of Tepexi, in Puebla state, specialized in the manufacture of these pots, which were distributed far and wide via Teotihuacán.

Teotihuacán's marketplace was probably situated in the Great Compound, on the opposite side of the Street of the Dead from the Ciudadela or Citadel in the centre of the city. Here merchants from near and far dealt in locally manufactured and imported goods, as well as raw materials such as marine shells, rubber, luxury feathers, cotton, magnetite, hematite and chert.

Groups of foreign merchants made their homes in this great metropolis. One part of the city has been dubbed the Merchants' Barrio by archaeologists, who found large amounts of pottery there from Veracruz and from Maya lands in northern Belize and the Yucatán peninsula. Another quarter was home to merchants from Oaxaca, who built tombs modelled exactly on those in their ancestral home of Monte Albán.

THE TRADE ROUTE

A major trade route, dubbed the Teotihuacán corridor by historians, connected the city to markets and sources of raw materials to the east and south. It left the city via its East Avenue and headed to Calpulalpán, in Tlaxcala, then south-east to Huamantla. Two branches left Huamantla, one heading east to Veracruz and the second turning south by way of Teotihuacán. On the route, passes and gateways allowed officials to regulate the movement of raw materials into Teotihuacán and manufactured artefacts on the way out of the city.

Farther afield, Teotihuacán set up a trading centre in Matacapán, situated in fertile land in southern Veracruz between the volcano of San Martin Tuxtla and the waters of Lake Catemaco. It was close to the coast and to rivers leading inland, and might well have controlled trade by sea for Teotihuacáno merchants. Matacapán, a source of kaolin, became a major production centre for fine paste pottery. Artisans also made elite products of the kind made in the 'mother city' of Teotihuacán. They lived in an apartment compound of the sort built in Teotihuacán. Farther south, Teotihuacán had prolonged trading and diplomatic links with Monte Albán in Oaxaca. Carvings at Monte Albán, including four stelae erected around the Main Plaza's South Platform, depict figures that scholars interpret as a record of peaceful visits by high-ranking Teotihuacános.

Teotihuacán had trading contacts as far afield as Kaminaljuyú in the Guatemala Valley and Tikal in the central Maya region. Archaeological evidence suggests

Right:
This evocative Teotihuacano mask has survived intact with its mould.

that traders from Teotihuacán may have become well established in an enclave at Kaminaljuyú. Some scholars have suggested that Teotihuacán used force against Kaminaljuyú, which sat on a trade route for valuable cacao beans and was situated close to a major source of obsidian. Perhaps the Teotihuacános attempted to gain a monopoly over mining and distribution of obsidian. A central area of Kaminaljuyú was reconstructed in Teotihuacáno architectural style.

Settlements to the west of Kaminaljuyú on the Pacific coastal plain probably also had close links with Teotihuacán in the cacao trade and may have been home to Teotihuacáno merchants. One settlement produced Teotihuacán-style ceramic ritual vessels. There was probably also direct trading contract between Teotihuacán and Tikal. After Tikal's victory over Uaxactún in AD378, the Maya of Tikal adopted the style of warrior-costume associated with Teotihuacán, and began to plan battle campaigns according to the cycle of Venus, following the Teotihuacáno tradition.

In other directions, Teotihuacán dominated the Valley of Mexico to the south-west, while to north and west the city's interests were confined to sourcing raw materials. Far to the north-west, the city established a settlement at Alta Vista, in the modern state of Zacatecas, to exploit its sources of jadeite, turquoise and precious green stones, flint, chert, hematite and malachite. The raw materials were taken back by porters to be worked in the city's workshops.

TRADING OVER GREAT DISTANCES

The pattern of long-distance trading established by the Olmecs and Teotihuacános continued into the era of the Aztecs. Throughout this vast time span, trade and exchange networks were also vibrant over small distances within the many regions of Mesoamerica. Short-range trade tended to be in foodstuffs and other everyday commodities such as clothing and household pottery, while long-range trade was in rare commodities highly prized for their use in religious ritual or as status symbols by members of the elite. Quetzal feathers – used in priestly and royal costumes – jaguar skins and sacred greenstones used for divine effigies and masks all commanded a high value at market.

MAYA CONNECTIONS

The Maya, who were in the path between the markets and raw materials of Central America and Mexican sites such as San Lorenzo, Teotihuacán, El Tajín or Tenochtitlán, played a crucial role in long-distance trade connections. Maya lands were also sources of prized commodities. Quetzal feathers, jadeite, serpentine, pyrite and obsidian were exported from the southern Maya highlands. Jaguar skins and teeth, valued for use in royal ceremonial, were exported from the lowlands of the central Maya region, together with parrot and macaw feathers. From coastal areas of the southern Maya region came sharks' teeth, coral, shells and sting-ray spines used for bloodletting in rites of autosacrifice, as well as cacao. Salt was traded from the coasts of Yucatán.

Below: Tarascan artisans made these lip ornaments from gold, obsidian and turquoise before 1500.

Above: Many goods travelled long distances on the Aztec tribute network. This codex page lists tribute from 16 imperial towns.

Merchants were trading over long distances from the central Maya region by at least 300BC. There were three principal routes through Maya lands. The northern way ran along the coast of Yucatán, the central route followed tracks and waterways through the lowlands of El Petén and the southern route came down the coastal plain adjoining the Pacific Ocean. Some traders followed the Usumacinta, Pasíon, Chixoy and other rivers southwards into the southern Maya highlands, and they were able to make their way through to the Motagua Valley and its path to the Gulf of Honduras. Within Maya territories, trade routes linked the northern parts of Yucatán with their salt industry and with the southern regions that were the important source of obsidian and quetzal feathers.

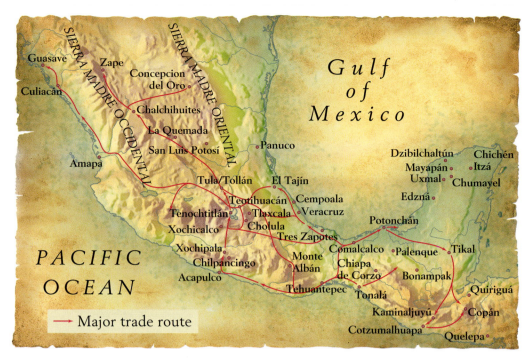

Above: Wherever possible, traders chose to follow low-lying routes through river valleys or along coastal plains.

Goods were laboriously transported by porters. Mesoamericans certainly knew how to make wheels, for they left wheeled toys in tombs, but they did not make wheeled vehicles for transport. In part this was because they lacked large traction animals but, in addition, many parts of Mesoamerica were unsuited to wheeled transport and more easily traversed on foot or by boat. A porter secured a load around his head or chest using rope and often travelled in convoy with several colleagues. In Aztec times the maximum load permitted was about 22kg (50lb) per person. Goods were also packed in great canoes and taken to sea or along rivers.

NORTHERN TRADE

In the north of Mexico, La Quemada (in modern Zacatecas state) lay in a good position for north–south trade, including turquoise from what is now the US state of New Mexico, and throve throughout the Classic Period until c.AD850. It is part of the Chalchihuite culture, whose remains provide early evidence of religious and military iconography (skull racks, *chacmools* and symbols of the god of the north, darkness and fate, Tezcatlipoca), which would become very important in Aztec times. In the far north, Casas Grandes, in modern Chihuahua state, was a major centre from c.1050, part of an important trading network linking Mesoamerica to sites in the south-west USA. Marine trade across the Caribbean also linked the islands and the south-east USA.

AZTEC TRADE ROUTES

In Aztec times, merchants doubtless operated from Tenochtitlán to the north, in the modern states of Zacatecas and Durango, and to the north-west in Querataro and Hidalgo, but historians know more about trade towards the

Right: Chachihuite settlements in northern Mexico combined fortified trading sites with farming villages and religious centres.

south. Routes from Tenochtitlán led down to Tuxtepec, where they divided, with one path leading into Oaxaca and on into the Isthmus of Tehuantepec and Soconusco, and one leading to the coast of the Gulf of Mexico and the towns of Coatzacoalco and, inland a little way, Cimatan.

From Cimatan traders could follow the River Grijalva into the Chiapas Highlands, where amber was to be found, or travel east into the region of Chontalapa, where there were no fewer than 25 Aztec trading posts with warehouses to store goods.

Beyond, on the Gulf coast, the port of Xicalango at the western edge of the Laguna de Terminos was almost certainly an Aztec trading centre, although it was peopled by Chontal-speaking Maya. From Xicalango, merchants could follow tracks

and waterways down to the forests of El Petén in the central Maya region and beyond to trading posts on the coast of the Caribbean Sea.

From Tenochtitlán, merchants exported luxury goods manufactured in the imperial capital from raw materials brought in by trade or as tribute from subject regions of the empire, as well as obsidian, bells and ornaments of copper, combs and herbs. Slaves were also exported to areas needing cheap labour such as cacao plantations on the coasts of the Gulf, the Pacific and the Caribbean. They imported cacao, gold, animal skins, precious stones and brightly coloured feathers.

BY CANOE AND PADDLE

In the 10th century, the powerful merchants of Chichén Itzá built a trading post on Isla Cerritos, a small island just off the coast of northern Yucatán and about 90km (55 miles) from their capital city. They built or improved existing piers and docks, together with a 330m (1,000ft) sea wall to guarantee calm waters for unloading from large seagoing canoes. These vessels, recently developed, transformed seagoing trade. At 15m (50ft) long and 2m (6ft 6in) wide, they were far bigger than earlier canoes and able to voyage into far rougher waters.

SEA TRADE

Through Isla Cerritos, Chichén Itzá imported basalt from Belize, gold jewellery from Central America, pottery from Guatemala and obsidian from sites in Mexico. Itzá sea traders travelled as far as the ports of Naco and Nito in Honduras.

Coastal settlements were probably operated in this way as trading posts for powerful inland cities or states throughout Mesoamerican history. For example, Cerros, on a peninsula of coastal Belize

Below: Caribbean waves wash the shore by the trading centre of Cozumel. Goats were traded by canoe along the coast and among offshore islands.

Above: Members of the merchant elite lived in the Palace of the Kings, a sumptuous residence in the trading city of Mayapán.

that projects into Chetumal Bay, was transformed from a small village into a significant settlement with large pyramids, public buildings and platforms in the period 50BC–AD100, probably at the behest of an inland centre seeking an outlet into the Caribbean Sea. The style

and appearance of the stucco deity-masks on these buildings suggest links to nearby Lamanai or, farther afield, to Tikal. Archaeological evidence has led historians to suggest that Cerros operated in tandem with Komchen, far away in northern Yucatán, as a trading partner, probably in the movement of salt from the northern region. Jade and obsidian from the southern Maya region were also traded at Cerros.

Mesoamericans carried on sea trade from earliest times. The peoples of western Mexico were in contact along the Pacific coast with tribes in Ecuador as early as 1500BC – as suggested by the appearance of Ecuadorian-style chamber tombs. In the Olmec centre at Teopantecuanitlán, in the Guerrero region, a workshop produced elite items using marine shells from distant points on the Pacific Coast.

TRADING POSTS

Many sites along the coasts of the Yucatán peninsula and Belize thrived through seagoing trade for many centuries. Jaina Island, the settlement off the west coast of the peninsula celebrated for its cemetery and the clay figures left in its graves, was a thriving trading and fishing port for at least 700 years. Tancah, a fortified town on the eastern coast of northern Yucatán,

Above: The elite of Yucatán combined warfare with trade. This is a mural in the Temple of the Warriors in Chichén Itzá.

Mayapán – Mayapán, Uxmal and a Chichén Itzá much reduced from its former independent glory – had control of seagoing trade, and probably built Tulum.

The League's merchant elite also maintained an offshore trading centre on the Isle of Cozumel, a little further north opposite the mainland settlement of Xcaret. On Cozumel, large platforms right across the island were used as seasonal stores for products such as honey, cacao and salt. The island traded all year in obsidian and building stone. The western part of Cozumel was the site of one of the region's most important religious shrines, to the Maya Moon Goddess Ix Chel.

Below: Lying in the sacred east, Tulum – together with Xelhá and Tancah – was a religious as well as a trading site. This structure is a clifftop temple to the wind god.

appears to have been a centre for trade in the *Strombus gigas*, a type of conch shell used in religious ritual from at least the time of Teotihuacán, where the shells are depicted in murals. Tancah was a trading post from the last centuries BC onwards, handling obsidian, jade, pyrite, granite and slate vessels exported from the Maya cities of the Puuc region inland. The neighbouring coastal settlement of Xelha was a port for the inland city of Cobá from at least the 10th century. A *sacbé* or raised causeway left the main square of Xelha and ran inland to Cobá.

CONTROL OF SEA TRADE

Around 6km (3½ miles) south along the coast lay Tulum, which was founded on the cliff top overlooking the Caribbean Sea in 1200 at a time when maritime commerce was a source of great wealth and prestige for the merchants of the northern Yucatán peninsula.

A cliff-top beacon guided sailors through a gap in the reef that runs parallel to the shore and on to a safe landing on the beach beneath the town. At this time, the cities of the League of

TRADERS, SPIES, PROTECTORS

Long-range trade in the Aztec empire was handled by professional merchants called *pochteca*. Working both on their own behalf and as emissaries of rulers and members of the nobility, they specialized in importing luxurious materials such as animal skins, rare feathers, precious shells and stones used in religious ritual. The Aztec word *pochteca* is derived from their name for the *Bombax ceiba*, the great tropical tree that was viewed by the ancient Mesoamericans as the tree of life that linked the terrestrial realm to heaven and to the underworld. The tree of life was an image for the king or rule, and the association of *pochteca* with the tree suggests that merchants were viewed – like kings – as protectors or guarantors of stability and fertility.

Left: This exquisite jade ear ornament, carved delicately with Maya glyphs, was found by archaeologists at Pomona, Belize.

MERCHANT WARDS

Pochteca were an elite hereditary group, whose members lived together as a *capultin* kin body in a part of the city reserved for them. Such was the size of Tenochtitlán and the number of *pochteca* serving the empire that there were six wards for merchants in the capital: Amachtlan, Atlauhco, Itztotolco, Pochtlán, Tepetitlán and Tzonmolco.

Ten other towns in the Valley of Mexico were renowned for their communities of professional merchants. These were: Azcapotzalco, Chalco, Coatlinchán, Cuauhtitlán, Huexotla, Huitzilopochco, Otumba, Mixcoac, Texcoco and Xochimilco.

There was a strict hierarchy among *pochteca*. The *pochtecatlatoque* were the most senior merchants, handpicked by the *tlatoani* and his advisers to organize trading expeditions and to supervize the activities of younger traders. They were proven merchants with wide experience of travel, usually drawn from the 'aristocracy' of trading families. The *pochtecatlatoque* stayed in Tenochtitlán and followed the progress of an expedition through reports sent back by the travelling merchants; both overseer and trader took a share in the profits. Perhaps most prestigious of all the responsibilities of the *pochtecatlatoque* was to ensure that the capital's markets were orderly and honest places. They sat in judgement on dishonest *pochteca* and customers in special merchants' courts and no other authority could interfere with or challenge their judgements. A trader found guilty of cheating or selling stolen goods or a person caught trying to steal would be sentenced to death.

SLAVE TRADERS

Second in the hierarchy of *pochteca* were traders in slaves. They were called *tlaltlani* ('washers of slaves'), a reference to the ritual bathing that slaves underwent before they were taken to be sacrificed. Bernardino de Sahagún recounts in his *General History of the Things of New Spain* that *tlaltlani* were the wealthiest of all merchants. By tradition they were particularly devout and were treated with the greatest respect as providers of sacrificial victims.

Beneath them were the travelling *pochteca*, the veterans of long-range expeditions who brought luxury produce back to Tenochtitlán's eager markets. They were sometimes called *oztomeca* ('front-line merchants'). Those among the *oztomeca* who worked only for the *tlatoani* were called *tencunenenque* ('king's voyagers'); they often worked as collectors of tribute from subject states within the empire.

Pochteca held a special position of privilege. Unlike their fellows, they were not required to perform personal services for the *tlatoani*. Instead they provided elite goods as tribute. In 1500, as a reward for the role played by *pochteca* in the military conquest of Soconusco, the *tlatoani* Ahuítzotl (r. 1486–1502) made a proclamation praising long-range merchants and granting them the right to wear loincloths and capes that were normally reserved for the nobility on special occasions.

SPIES BEHIND ENEMY LINES

One group of merchants, the *naualoz-tomeca* ('traders in disguise'), performed a vital function for the *tlatoani*, his military advisers and the army commanders. Wherever they went, ostensibly travelling as merchants, they were working as spies, looking for signs of potential unrest and listening for mutterings of discontent against the Aztec rulers. When the military elite in Tenochtitlán was planning a military campaign, it would send *naualoztomeca* into the region to seek useful preliminary information.

In the early Aztec era, traveller-spies went through the empire disguised as locals in order to learn what they could from gossip in the marketplace. However, later the travellers began to take the guise of merchants. It was a dangerous occupation; if caught, a spy was likely to be slain and perhaps cooked. Upon landing in Mexico, Hernán Cortés made first contact with a group of *naualoztomeca*. It was these trader-spies who carried the first news of strange bearded beings in 'flying' ships back to the court of Moctezuma II in Tenochtitlán.

NOBLE MAYA TRADERS

The Aztecs' Maya contemporaries did not have professional merchants comparable to the *pochteca*. Among the Maya, long-distance trade was carried out by rulers and members of the nobility. At Chichén Itzá and Mayapán, the rulers appear to have been merchants. One account of the fall of Mayapán recounts that all the city's rulers were slaughtered in an attack, save one who was away from the city on his travels, seeking trade.

In both Maya and Aztec lands, short-distance trading was performed either by small-scale entrepreneurs, peddlers who bought and sold as they travelled hither and

Right: Danger on the road. A detail from the Codex Mendoza *shows Aztec trader-spies being attacked by lawless locals.*

thither, or by the producers and manufacturers of the goods – the farmers, weavers, toolmakers and potters. From ancient times, across Mesoamerica, long-distance trade was the preserve of a wealthy ruling elite. Trade was the lifeblood of development: because they brought wealth to the community, and because they traded in

Above: The largest of these vases from Tikal shows a fat Maya merchant who was clearly wealthy enough to indulge himself.

elite goods such as feathers, jaguar skins and sacrificial knives that were needed for religious ceremony, traders began to enjoy religious prestige.

MARKETS LARGE AND SMALL

The Aztec capital contained several outdoor markets of various sizes. (The outdoor marketplace was called *tianquiztli* in Nahuatl.) In addition to the justly celebrated marketplace in Tlatelolco, there was another substantial market in Tenochtitlán proper, alongside the ceremonial precinct. There were also many smaller places of sale scattered throughout the city in its various wards.

WHO SOLD WHAT, WHEN

The sale of elite goods that had been transported from distant parts of the empire was probably restricted to the Tlatelolco and the main Tenochtitlán market. Sales in the different wards were probably of local agricultural produce brought in from *chinampa* fields or of craft products made at workshops in the vicinity. Transactions at these markets were not purely economic, but were bound into the fabric of life and

Above: The walls, steps and frieze carving are part of the vast Pyramid of Quetzalcóatl in Cholula, a town sacred to that god.

Right: These steps and walls are another part of the pyramid remains at Cholula, a major trading as well as a religious centre.

intimately connected with entertainment, socializing, politics and religion. Markets were places where people made friends, swapped news and gossip, perhaps hatched plots and formed alliances, places through which people made their way to the temple.

It is possible that market days were scheduled to coincide with important days in the ritual calendar. Pilgrims would have travelled to a town to make offerings at its shrine and then gone on to the marketplace. Merchants would have taken part in the pilgrimage.

RELIGION AND COMMERCE

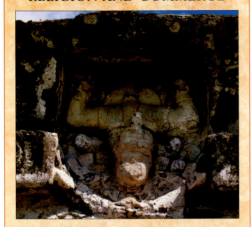

Above: The Descending God, Tulum.

Many Mesoamerican trading settlements were also important religious centres. In the highlands of Mexico, Cholula's marketplace was thronged with people while the city's great Temple of Quetzalcóatl was a major draw for pilgrims.

Several trading sites on the eastern seaboard of the Yucatán peninsula were believed to have sacred power because of their position towards the direction of the moon's rising and the reappearance of Venus. The Isle of Cozumel, an important trading port for the League of Mayapán, contained a shrine to moon goddess Ix Chel on its eastward-facing shore; the goddess was believed to speak through an oracle there. On the mainland, the fortified trading centre at Tancah was the site of a *cenote* or large natural well with a holy cave lying on an east–west axis and painted with murals delineating the fearful power of the sea. At nearby Tulum, the Temple of the Descending God was adorned with a carving of a creature diving towards earth; the curious image, only found at Tulum and Cobá, is thought to be associated with the cult of the planet Venus in the form of Xux Ek, the Maya 'wasp star' god.

It is likely that the holy day was enjoyed as a holiday, with entertainments and perhaps a ball game tournament.

Some markets specialized in local produce. Cholula, for example, won a wide reputation for the excellence of its chillies, while Coyoacán was known for the wood grown near the town. Fine gourds, cloth and ceramics were the speciality of Texcoco market. The best places to go for slaves were Azcapotzalco and Itzocán, and the best dog market was at Acolman. In the Mixtec area, the market at Miahuatlán was widely renowned, not least for its sale of exquisite local gold work. Smaller markets were usually held each day or sometimes on a rota with other nearby centres.

MAYA MARKETS

Many Maya towns and cities also held centralized markets in open squares. There is little archaeological evidence of marketplaces, however. Commercial activity usually took place in the open, with perhaps a few pole-and-thatch buildings to provide shade or to keep the rain off, that have since decayed. There is evidence that Classic Period Tikal had a permanent central marketplace. Archaeologists believe that the commercial zone was probably an enclosed area of the city's East Plaza, containing buildings with many doorways. We know that in the post-Classic Period, Iximche in the southern Maya region had a market plaza with overseers to settle arguments, ensure that regulations were observed and levy taxes. As at Tlatelolco, Maya markets were efficiently organized, with different types of goods laid out in separate areas.

Markets contained areas for visiting and foreign merchants, but rival controlling interests sometimes came into opposition. For example, Aztec *pochteca* trading in elite goods were not welcome in areas where Maya nobles ran long-distance trade. Where necessary, representatives of the two sides met in neutral areas.

Below: At Tollán, the remains of the Palacio Quemado lie to the west of the raised temple platform sacred to Quetzalcóatl.

THE GREAT MARKET AT TLATELOLCO

The greatest marketplace of the Aztec empire was at Tlatelolco, the island city that adjoined the imperial capital of Tenochtitlán. Even on a quiet day, 25,000 people would throng the Tlatelolco marketplace, according to the conquistador Anónimo, while every five days a special market attracted more than double that number. Hernán Cortés declared that he saw around 60,000 people in the market. His colleague Bernal Díaz reported that even in the course of two days a curious person would not be able to see the vast range of produce sold there.

The market square at Tlatelolco was surrounded by a covered arcade. In its centre stood a raised platform from which officials made public pronouncements and where thieves and dishonest merchants were shamed and put to death by stoning. The traders' stalls were arranged in a grid pattern around the central platform. At one corner of the market square was the court of the *pochtecatlatoque*, the most senior merchants whose responsibility was to levy sales taxes, to maintain order in the marketplace and also to sit in judgement on those who broke the law.

Above: This illustration, from the Florentine Codex, *is of Aztecs storing amaranth.*

The goods were laid out in areas according to type. The *pochtecatlatoque* organized the market, ensuring products were sold in the right area and at the right price. Every raw material and product imaginable, the produce of a great empire, was available in the Tlatelolco market.

ANCIENT CORNUCOPIA

A canal ran down one side of the marketplace, and a stream of heavily laden porters carried goods from canoes to market stalls. In one area were farmers and merchants selling fresh

Left: These jewellery pieces are typical of the artefacts the elite could buy at Tlatelolco.

produce: beans, vegetables, herbs and fruits. In another were turkeys, deer, ducks, rabbits, dogs and hares. Elsewhere, a customer could find fish and all kinds of marine life; in another place, tortillas, honey cakes and other cooked foods were on offer, including, according to the conquistador Bernal Díaz, cakes with the flavour of cheese made by fisherwomen using a weed that grows in Lake Texcoco.

In another part of the market, shoppers could browse among a vast range of pots, plates, water jars and bowls before moving on to look for bark paper and inks, then to seek out reeds filled with tobacco. A person could buy sandals, coloured robes and lengths of plain cloth. Another could buy timber or pine torches. Those seeking elite items would find them in plentiful supply: feathers of many colours, including the magnificent quetzal tail feathers of up to 1m (more than 3ft) in length; the skins of jaguars, lions and deer; magnificent gold masks and jewellery fashioned by the best Mixtec goldsmiths; delicately finished mosaic masks; elegant sacrificial knives; statues, and other stone carvings; turquoise, jade and other precious stones. A warrior could find all kinds of military equipment, including padded cotton armour, leather shields, the sharpest *atlatl* darts of obsidian and splendid ceremonial cloaks and shields decorated with feathers and mosaic.

Slaves were also for sale. Merchants fitted them with collars and bound them to a long pole to prevent them running away. Any slaves who did escape could gain their freedom if they managed to reach the palace of the *tlatoani* without being caught. Only the merchant who owned them could give chase. Some merchants bought slaves to offer as sacrifices, particularly for the festival of Panquetzalíztli ('Lifting of the Banners'), which was held after the harvest each year. Others purchased strong male slaves to transport and sell to cacao plantations or as canoe oarsmen in coastal regions. Some female slaves were

sold as prostitutes. The going rate for a slave was 25 cotton cloaks, rising to 35 cloaks for one who was skilled in dancing.

All goods were counted out or sold by measuring their size, never by weight. Customers usually bartered with merchants, although some products, such as cacao beans, cotton mantles, pieces of tin, copper axe-blades, transparent quills full of gold dust and the feathers of tropical birds, were used as forms of currency.

PUNISHMENTS AND PROCESSIONS

Cheats sometimes got away with making counterfeit cacao beans from amaranth dough and wax. When the *pochtecatlatoque* found a merchant guilty of trying to cheat his customers they sentenced him to be put to death on the platform in the centre of the square. The merchant's goods were

confiscated and his dishonest measures smashed. A person caught stealing from a stall or storehouse would be similarly sentenced to death.

The marketplace was a vibrant place where people gathered to chat, street performers entertained the crowds and drummers set bystanders dancing. Religious processions passed through the market from the ceremonial precinct of Tlatelolco nearby. Priests waving smoking censers, their bodies painted black and long hair matted with sacrificial blood, made an unnerving spectacle. Sometimes they were at the head of a procession of victims bound for sacrifice in the temple.

Below: Today office buildings crowd close to excavated ruins of Tlatelolco platforms in the heart of the Mexican capital.

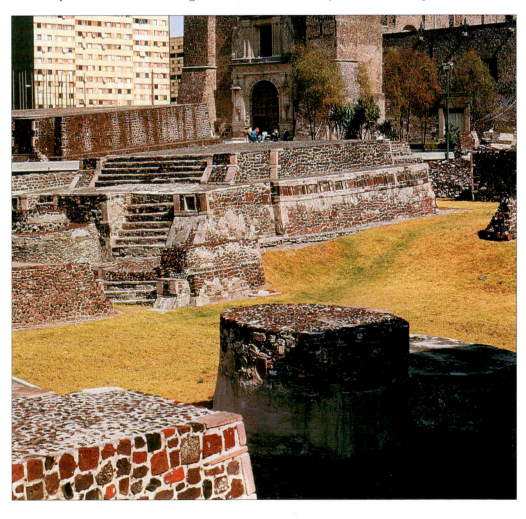

A NETWORK OF TRIBUTE

Large quantities of produce entered Tenochtitlán in the form of tribute payments from provinces within the Aztec empire. The activities of tribute collectors complemented those of *pochteca* merchants in providing sumptuous goods to please the nobles of the imperial capital and to supply the materials used in the city's magnificent religious ceremonies.

A TRIBUTARY EMPIRE

Some *pochteca* worked as itinerant tribute collectors, but generally collectors were appointed to reside in a conquered territory to ensure payments were made. The Triple Alliance of Tenochtitlán, Texcoco and Tlacopán built its tributary empire through military might: its armies pursued battle to the point at which a conquered state or city agreed to pay tribute, when the conquerors imposed a schedule of amounts and timings. The rulers of the defeated state remained in power, and the collector made sure that they honoured the tribute agreement, under threat of further military action.

Tribute payments maintained the infrastructure and daily operations of the empire. Some provinces were required to send labourers for construction projects, others tools and building materials, some

Below: The Zapotecs of Monte Albán celebrated their conquest-led tribute network in carvings on the arrow-shaped Building J.

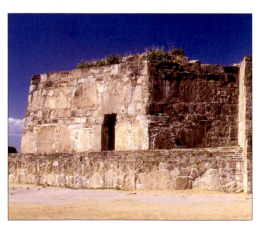

sent soldiers, others military equipment such as shields and padded cotton war jerkins. Many areas sent maize, beans and other basic foodstuffs, while others provided firewood for the braziers of the nobility. Certain states were contracted to send local products such as obsidian or cacao, fine metalwork or ceramics, jaguar skins or colourful feathers. One of the most highly prized Aztec tributary provinces was the resource-rich region of Soconusco, defeated after four years' conflict by Ahuítzotl in 1486; it provided tribute of jaguar skins and jewellery.

RECORDS OF PAYMENT

Details of the tribute network operated by Texcoco are found in the 16th-century document the *Mapa Quinatzin*. They show how meticulously tribute operations were planned. There were eight tributary regions, each with its own tribute collector required, among other responsibilities, to furnish the administrative buildings, city temples and royal palaces in Texcoco with foodstuffs and wood for braziers. In particular, two groups of 13 tributary towns were arranged in a rota to provide firewood for the *tlatoani*'s main palace throughout the year. The *Codex Mendoza* (*c.*1541) contains a lengthy tribute list detailing the responsibilities throughout the year of various tributary towns and states. Cuauhnahuac is listed as one of 16 towns contracted to dispatch a consignment of cotton skirts, loincloths and robes to Tenochtitlán twice a year, supplemented by an annual delivery of shields and war equipment. With so many tribute payers required to provide materials according to a regular schedule, there must have been a steady stream of porters and canoes bringing deliveries from far and wide, which would have required detailed administrative control.

Before the Triple Alliance, other cultures – including the Zapotecs of Monte Albán and the Toltecs of Tollán – established tributary empires. At Monte

Above: Portable wealth. This pendant earring of solid gold was one of the pieces found in Monte Albán Tomb 7 in 1932.

Right: A page from the Codex Mendoza *shows the tribute collected by Aztec civil servants from the province of Tochtepec.*

Albán, the curious arrow-shaped structure known to archaeologists as Building J, erected between *c.*200BC and AD300 in the Main Plaza, bears about 50 carvings that appear to represent areas conquered or required to pay tribute to the Zapotecs. Some carvings specify the kind of tribute that must be paid.

They included Cuicatlán, a mountain settlement on the border between Oaxaca and the Téhuacan Valley, and Tututepec on the coast of the Pacific Ocean. At Cuicatlán the Zapotecs acted with great ruthlessness: they destroyed entire villages, moved other settlements, established military strongholds and terrified surviving locals by building skull racks in their villages to display the heads of their conquered menfolk.

In many areas they did not need to use military force, however. In return for supplying elite goods from Monte Albán to the leading figures of a village, the Zapotecs exacted an agreement that they would receive tribute of agricultural produce. Many centuries later, the warriors of Xochicalco, in the western part of Morelos, established a tributary empire in the period AD700–900, as evidenced by glyphs of tribute-paying towns carved on the upper part of the Pyramid of the Feathered Serpent there.

The Putún Maya traders who ruled Chichén Itzá and later Mayapán both built tribute networks. At Mayapán, cotton, copal, cacao, honey and turkeys were among the forms of tribute received. In the southern Maya realm the warlike Quiché Maya also exacted tribute payments from those they conquered. However, the Quiché did not allow local leaders to remain in place, as the Aztecs did; instead, triumphant warlords had their enemies executed and took the dead men's wives into their own families.

THE GIVING OF GIFTS

From earliest times goods moved across Mesoamerica in the form of gifts between elite groups in different areas. Such gift-giving was a mark of mutual respect between rulers and a way of sharing resources between regions rich in different source materials – for instance, a highland group might make a gift of obsidian cutting blades in return for surplus maize or cacao grown by another group in the coastal lowlands. The gift of sumptuous and prestigious materials was also a statement of power on behalf of the giver, an attempt to demonstrate status. Moctezuma II attempted to prove his divine grandeur and magnificence by making splendid gifts of gold, silver and magnificent featherwork to Hernán Cortés and the conquistadors in 1519.

THE SACRED WAY

The Maya built raised causeways known as *sacbeob* (singular: *sacbé*) between settlements. These paved roads eased communications and passage for merchants while giving solid form to political alliances among cities.

GREAT CAUSEWAY

The greatest of these roads was built *c.*AD800 in Yucatán, and ran for 100km (60 miles) from the Castillo pyramid at Cobá to Yaxuná. Cobá lay at the intersection of some 43 roads. It was also connected, for example, to its seaport at Xelhá. Some scholars believe that the rulers of Cobá embarked on this remarkable feat of engineering in an attempt to consolidate their power at a time when the aggressive Putún Maya incomers at Chichén Itzá were making unwelcome intrusions into the region. The attempt may have succeeded: the Itzá attacked and defeated Yaxuná in *c.*AD850, but there is no evidence they overcame Cobá. Its people maintained their independence, although the city's trading success was limited, its ambitious building programmes were curtailed and various outer parts of the settlement were gradually abandoned.

Several *sacbeob* were constructed in northern Yucatán. Typically they were elevated 2.5m (8ft) above the surround-

Above: Several causeways were in use at the fortified trading centre at La Quemada in Zacatecas state, Mexico.

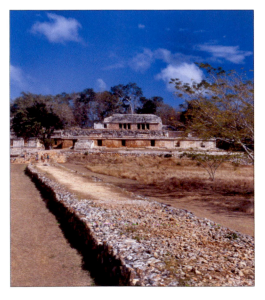

Left: A sacbé *connects a small group of buildings to the two-storey palace at Labná. The palace is similar to that at Sayil.*

ing land, were around 4.5m (15ft) wide and covered with lime cement. Labourers used a 5-ton roller to finish the surface; this would have needed 15 workers to push it. The roads did not curve: they ran perfectly straight, then made a sudden turn to change direction if necessary. One – 4m (13ft) wide – ran for 18km (11 miles) between Uxmal and Kabah. At Kabah it passed through a remarkable stone corbelled arch with a span of 5m (16ft) and led to the central civic area. Another ran for 18km from the settlement at Ucí. It was a remarkable 8m (26ft) wide.

The Maya built *sacbeob* from the time they erected their first monumental buildings in the lowlands. The earliest known system links El Mirador to Nakbé, 13km (8 miles) away, Tintal and other nearby sites. These roads were built in the Late Preclassic Period (*c.*400BC–AD250). The *sacbeob* between cities were expanded versions of the sacred ways that the Maya built to link areas within their

cities. At El Mirador, causeways connected different parts of the city centre. A series of *sacbeob* ran from the Great Plaza in the centre of Tikal. One led north, to the buildings labelled Pyramid Group 3D-2 and Group H by archaeologists. Another went directly west to Temple IV and a third ran south-east to the Temple of Inscriptions. At Chichén Itzá a stone *sacbé* 6m (20ft) wide and 300m (985ft) long connected the Temple of the Feathered Serpent to the Sacred cenote.

SACRED SYMBOLISM

The causeways in cities such as Tikal were integrated into the sacred symbolism of the site layout. The arcane meaning of the layout was that the north was the realm of supernaturals, glorious deceased ancestors who had risen to the heavens, while the south was the region of the Underworld. A ball court was often built between north and south to represent an entrance to the Underworld. Buildings to the east and west suggested the east–west passage of the sun and the rule of the king, whose symbol was the sun.

Causeways were used to link different symbolic areas and to emphasize the unity of the design. At Tikal, for example, the sacred north position was filled both by the North Acropolis, which contained many tombs of ancestors, and further out by the Pyramid Group 3D-2. South was the South Acropolis, west was Temple IV and east was the Temple of the Inscriptions. The three causeways completed the design. A ball court in the East Plaza was an additional way into the Underworld between north and south.

In many cities, for example Yaxhá and Caracol, causeways were built to lead out from the centre to outer settlements. At Caracol there were no fewer than seven causeways providing access from the centre to living areas and plazas, with one running for 8km (5 miles) to the allied smaller settlement at Cahal Pichik. At Seibal the three main groups of buildings were laid out on a cluster of hilltops and connected to one another by causeways. A few *sacbeob* were built in other parts

Below: Archaeologists have dated this well-preserved roadway at Cantona in Puebla state to AD700–950.

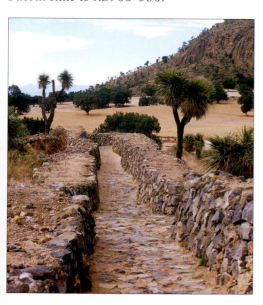

of Mesoamerica. At Xochicalco, paved causeways like *sacbeob* were the connecting link between different parts of the ancient city. In northern Mexico the trading settlement of La Quemada, in southern Zacatecas state, also used causeways to link different parts of the settlement.

AZTEC ROADS
There is little archaeological evidence of Aztec roads. Whereas in Maya lands labourers built paved *sacbeob*, in southern and central highland Mesoamerica there was generally no need to build formal roads between settlements. However, scholars know that a network of routes carried trade within the Aztec empire.

Above: The carving on the façade of the Governor's Palace at Uxmal is reproduced in Catherwood's 1841 drawing. From Uxmal a sacbé *ran directly to Kabah, where it passed beneath an archway.*

There are references in post-Conquest accounts to roads, roadside gods, rest houses and teams of couriers and there was certainly a road inland from Veracruz to Tenochtitlán, for Cortés followed it in 1519. Aztec *pochteca* followed well-trodden paths with their long caravans of human porters, heavily laden with goods, or had their loads transferred to canoes for transport by river and in coastal waters. Aztec garrisons were established at vulnerable points on the trade routes.

CHAPTER FOUR

THE WORLD OF WORK

Opportunities for Mesoamericans were limited by birth. We know this from Spanish records about the Aztecs, their contemporaries and the Maya in the 16th century. Also, because the archaeological record of preceding Mesoamerican cultures is similar to that of the Aztec and Maya and indicates that there was continuous development, we can project the nature of Aztec society back into pre-Aztec times. The top military, legal, administrative and priestly positions were open only to members of the hereditary nobility; among the middle class of skilled artisans and merchants, most were probably glad to follow their family profession, since it could provide sufficient wealth to secure a good level of comfort. Most people had their living from the land, the men working as fishermen, hunters and farmers.

In terms of food and basics, common people could be self-sufficient. They grew most, if not all, of the food they ate. They often had sufficient skills to produce pots, clothing, basketwork and tools for their own use. Some might produce a surplus of cloth or tools that could be bartered for luxury items – a turkey, some meat or extra vegetables, decorated clothing and so on – at market. They were also connected to the wider world of religious life, ceremonial centres and military campaigns through their responsibilities to pay taxes or tribute to their rulers and to serve in the army or as labourers in construction projects when required.

Left: A codex scene depicts the harvesting of cacao. Farming was the principal livelihood of most Mesoamericans.

RAISING CROPS ON LAND AND WATER

At Tenochtitlán farmers relied on *chinampa* fields in Lake Texcoco. The first *chinampas* were constructed along the shore or around islands, but by the reign of Moctezuma I, water control techniques made it possible to reclaim fields from the lake.

CREATING CHINAMPAS

A farmer building a *chinampa* plot would ideally use a shallow or swampy part of the lake. First he would mark out a rectangular area around 30m (100ft) long and 2.5m (8ft) across with four corner posts, then build fences around the area with wattles, vegetation and mud. He or a member of his kin group could make another *chinampa* directly alongside the first, with a canal running between the two, and proceeding in this way the farmers of Tenochtitlán could create large areas of *chinampas* on a grid pattern. In some areas the *chinampas* were laid out in pairs between canals, with a footpath running between the two *chinampa* 'fields'. Some *chinampas* were very much

Above: One of several scenes of agricultural life in the Florentine Codex *of c. 1570 depicts Aztec farmers harvesting maize.*

bigger than the plot of 75sq m described, and could be as large as 850sq m (9,000sq ft); plots such as this supported as many as 15 farmers.

Farmers would plant willows at the edges of their plots. Their roots grew down into the lakebed and strengthened the walls. The trees required regular pruning to prevent them casting shade on the crops. The 'fields' within the fences were built up with layers of fertile sediment dredged from the lakebed. Farmers turned the earth with a hand-held implement and planted seeds in holes made with a planting stick or *coa*. In the dry season, farmers lifted water in a container from the canal onto the *chinampa* alongside. To fertilize the earth they used human excrement, which was carried by canoe from the city along the network of canals. Springs from the Ajusco mountains fed into lakes Chalco and Xochimilco, where great expanses of *chinampa* fields lay. The Aztecs needed to control the supply of water to prevent flooding in the wet season or drought in the dry period. They created a system of dams, canals and sluices – channels with end-gates that could be lifted or dropped to control the flow of water.

The main crops grown by the Aztecs were maize, beans, squashes, tomatoes and chillies. Farmers in Chalco and Tlaxcala grew large amounts of maize, and these areas became associated with the staple crop in Aztec times. Elsewhere other *chinampa* farmers in the Valley of Mexico grew vegetables and flowers.

BURNING FIELDS

In other parts of Mesoamerica, farmers used a range of agricultural methods, according to local conditions. In highland areas, which usually had mineral-rich soil, they cut terraces from the steep hillsides

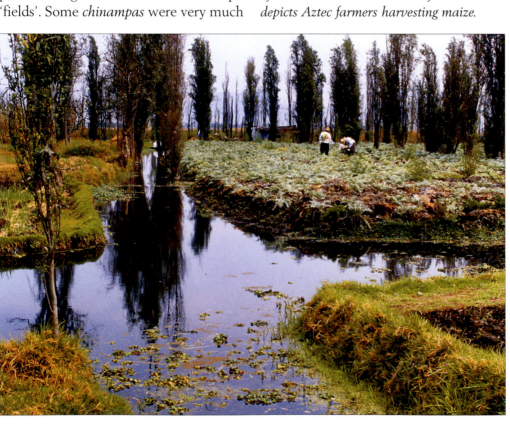

Left: Chinampa fields at Xochimilco, constructed by Aztecs in the 15th century, are still in use by Mexicans today.

Above: The method of building up a chinampa *field using stakes and mud is seen in this painting based on a 16th-century manuscript.*

and built aqueducts to irrigate the fields from mountain streams. In the tropical lowlands of the central Maya region, where soils were poorer, farmers practised 'slash-and-burn', first cutting down the dense jungle growth with stone axes, then leaving the plants to dry before burning them to enrich the soil and recover its fertility. They could use a field so made for perhaps three years, but then had to leave it fallow for as long as eight years to allow the soil to become enriched with minerals once more. Many farmers using this method then moved on to clear another area.

Where possible, lowland and other Maya agriculturalists also cut terraced fields, which helped to prevent water draining from the soil. They also made raised fields in swampy ground. The farmers cut channels in the wet ground and piled up the cleared earth, creating raised fields intersected with waterways for irrigation. Maya farmers were growing food on raised fields beside the Hondo river in Belize as

early as 1100BC. The method was also used in the Quintana Roo area of Yucatán and alongside the Candelaria river in Campeche. In Belize, humidity and high rainfall allowed farmers to grow highly valued crops of cacao, as well as cotton. At Pulltrouser Swamp in Belize, locals grew cacao, cotton, amaranth and maize on their raised-field agricultural land.

In the Maya lowlands, farmers planted maize, squash and beans together. The squash vines helped to prevent soil erosion, while the beans climbed the tall stalks of the corn. As in Tenochtitlán's *chinampa* fields, farmers turned earth using hand-held implements, then used a planting stick to make holes and dropped five or six seeds into each hole.

People kept kitchen gardens close to their houses: here they planted vegetables and the breadnut tree, which yields a fruit high in vegetable protein that can be stored without decaying for as long as 18 months. They may have grown fields of ramon, sapodilla, avocado and cacao.

FEEDING AN EXPANDING CITY

By the mid-1400s Tenochtitlán's population had grown to upwards of 150,000 – five times larger than its lakeside near-neighbour Texcoco, which had some 20–30,000 inhabitants. The Aztec capital, which did not have its own zone of *chinampa* fields, had a pressing need for more agricultural land. The *tlatoani* or ruler Itzcóatl seized control of the *chinampa* zone in the southern lakes, Chalco and Xochimilco. In the reign of Moctezuma I, sizeable new areas of *chinampa* were created in the lakebed. Imperial conquests also helped, by bringing substantial quantities of staple and luxury foods in the form of tribute payments from conquered regions.

GARDEN EXPERTS

In Aztec Tenochtitlán there was a hierarchy among agriculturalists. The men who worked the fields had a wide variety of skills and knowledge: they took responsibility for turning the soil, weeding, levelling land, measuring out fields, planting, watering by hand and using irrigation systems, harvesting and storing produce. However, there was also a group of experts in horticulture, widely respected for their knowledge in seeding and transplanting. These men were valued for their skills by members of the nobility and the political and priestly hierarchies. Combining their knowledge with information from the sacred *tonalamatl* calendar books, the garden experts decided the most propitious and the most practical times for sowing crops and harvesting them.

PLEASURE GARDENS

Garden experts were also much in demand for planning and maintaining the gardens of the empire. Many of the villas of Tenochtitlán had splendid pleasure gardens. Moctezuma II kept three: at his palace in Tenochtitlán, at Chapultepec and at Ixtapalapa. When the conquistador Bernal Díaz visited Moctezuma's garden at Ixtapalapa, he was astonished by the variety of trees, fruits and flowers and their captivating aromas. He declared there was probably no land on earth to match the one that contained such a garden. Hernán Cortés also visited the garden and described it in a 1520 letter to Carlos V of Spain as containing many trees, flowers and places for bathing, with an orchard and areas of aromatic herbs and a wide walkway around a central pool containing fish and visited by waterfowl.

At Texcotzingo, Netzahualcóyotl of Texcoco followed an established Aztec tradition in keeping a botanical garden. The most splendid of these botanical gardens was that founded in 1467 by Moctezuma I of Tenochtitlán in a warm, fertile spot at Huaxtepec, beneath Mount Popocatépetl in the modern Mexican state of Morelos.

When the Aztecs discovered an ancient garden created by their forerunners at Huaxtepec, Moctezuma appointed an official named Pinotetl to upgrade and revamp the already elaborate irrigation works, which included springs, reservoirs and fountains. Then the *tlatoani* ordered the transport from Cuetlaxtlán in Veracruz of cacao trees, vanilla orchid plants and other rare species and for herbs, cypresses and other plants from far-flung parts of the Aztec empire. The plants were carefully dug up, wrapped in cloth and sent to Huaxtepec along with experts in their cultivation.

Religious ceremonies were held to bless the plants and the enterprise. The specialist gardeners from far and wide joined in an eight-day fast before taking part in a bloodletting ceremony in which they pierced their earlobes and sprinkled the blood over the plants. Priests made offerings of incense and sacrificed a large number of quail in order to bless the earth with the birds' blood. These ceremonies must have won the gods' approval for

Left: Tribute sent to Tenochtitlán by Cihuatlan, on the coast, included cacao beans and rare seashells used in ritual.

Above: This 16th-century manuscript juxtaposes drawings showing the medicinal uses of various plants used by Mesoamericans with a picture of an Aztec god.

the plants took to their new home and grew fast and strong. When finished, Moctezuma's gardens – 11km (7 miles) in circumference – contained more than 2,000 species of herbs, shrubs and trees. It also contained an aviary and a zoo.

HEALING HERBS

In the botanical gardens at Huaxtepec and Texcotzingo, the garden experts grew a wide range of medicinal herbs. The use of healing herbs was an ancient Mesoamerican art. Most people knew enough to treat themselves and grew herbs among the vegetables on their garden plots. Some of the herbs grown in the botanical gardens were used in doctors' experiments. Members of the nobility paid for the experiments, in return for medical treatment when

needed. Ordinary citizens were able to volunteer as guinea pigs, receiving free experimental treatment on condition that they return to report the results to the doctors and planting experts.

THE MAYA AND CACAO

Foremost among elite crops grown by the Maya was cacao. To flourish, cacao needs a thick layer of good soil and humidity in all seasons. One of the prime exports from Maya lands to Mexico, it was grown in plantations, primarily in Soconusco (the Pacific coastal region of Guatemala and Chiapas), in the valley of the River Motagua and at sites in Belize.

The Maya merchant god Ek Chuah – known as god M by some scholars – was lord of cacao and the owners of plantations made offerings to him in the 15th month, Muan. According to the account given by

Right: This Maya chocolate pot was made c. AD300–900. It was used to pour the chocolate drink to generate a pleasing froth.

Diego de Landa of Maya religious festivals in 16th-century Yucatán, the plantation owners found a dog with cacao-coloured dots on his coat to kill and, amid the burning of incense also offered sacrifices of blue bird feathers and blue-coloured iguanas. To conclude the rite, each plantation owner was given a cacao pod to hold.

FRESH FROM THE WILD

Throughout their history Mesoamericans supplemented their diet with meat and fish. In the earliest days, hunting-gathering groups were self-sufficient, but as village life developed, people increasingly had specialized occupations and markets sprang up at which villagers could barter and exchange foods and other necessities. Skilled hunters doubtless brought their meat to market. Fishermen or traders carried dried fish from coastal, riverside or lakeside areas to inland settlements.

MAYA HUNTERS

Among the Maya, hunters used snares and traps to catch deer for their meat. They also hunted rabbits, pig-like mammals called peccaries and rodents – including squirrels, porcupines, agouti and paca. They were skilled with the blowpipe, sending tiny clay pellets at velocity to kill monkeys, macaws, raccoons and other animals in their habitat in the branches. In coastal, lakeside and riverside areas Maya fishermen thrived, using dugout canoes, nets and lines with bone fishhooks. All around the coasts of Maya lands and inland on freshwater lakes and rivers, fish and shellfish were an important part of the diet.

The Maya also domesticated and raised some animals. They kept dogs as guards and hunting companions and may also have fattened some for food. They also kept turkeys, doves – and perhaps

Above: Mesoamericans knew the coyote for its cunning and ability as a night hunter. This statue was made c.1250–1450.

the Muscovy duck – to eat. According to some authorities, the Maya raised herds of domesticated deer in large fenced areas for food. Describing the Maya of Yucatán in the 16th century, Bishop Diego de Landa reported that the women made a habit of breastfeeding young deer, who became entirely tame. In areas such

as the lands beside the Candelaria river in Campeche, the Maya might also have 'farmed' fish and molluscs in the waterways between their raised fields and in artificial ponds. They might have introduced freshwater fish into these enclosed areas of water and caught the excess produced by breeding.

De Landa also reported that Maya hunters in Yucatán believed that success in tracking, catching and killing animals was in the gift of the hunting gods Acanum and Suhui Dzipitabai. He reported that in the second and third month of the year, Uo and Zip, hunters partook in ceremonies honouring the gods. In waterside areas they were joined by fishermen praising the fishing deities Ah Kak Nexoy, Ah Pua, Ah Cit and Dzamal Cum. They prayed for success in the field. In the eleventh month, Zac, hunters celebrated another festival in honour of Acanum and Suhui Dzipitabai, this time seeking forgiveness for the blood they had spilled in the hunt. To the Maya, shedding blood was always a wicked act, for which a man or woman must seek forgiveness. Sacrificial offerings of one's own or a victim's blood were excepted.

IN HIGHLAND MEXICO

In Aztec times, the inhabitants of Tenochtitlán and other cities around the lakes of the Valley of Mexico had easy access to fish, shellfish and aquatic birds. Boys often hunted for birds with nets on the end of long poles while their fathers fished with canoes and nets on the waters of the lake. The men were also skilled in catching frogs and iguanas, a kind of lizard, for food. They collected *axolotl* newts, which were abundant in the lakes and were highly prized as a food and medicine. Many people kept small, hairless dogs as companions and pets – and as a

Left: In a scene from the Florentine Codex, an Aztec seated on a reed mat eyes the turkey and dogs he keeps for meat.

Above: A detail from a Maya mural depicts scenes of village life including fishing, hunting and digging the house garden.

source of food. Otherwise, animal meat was available at market, from local hunters, from traders and as part of the regular and substantial deliveries of tribute from around the empire. Diego Durán's account of the myriad kinds of tribute delivered to Tenochtitlán listed deer, rabbits, quails, weasels, moles, snakes and rats as well as larger animals including jaguars and ocelots.

From ancient times, the Aztecs' fore-runners and ancestors in Mexico had hunted in small bands by tracking and trapping. They used chipped flint and obsidian weapons such as spears and *atlatl* darts to kill mammoths and other large game, but also trapped and hunted many other small creatures including turtles, birds, rabbits and gophers. The Aztec god of hunting, Mixcóatl, probably originated in these archaic times as a hurricane or storm god. His name means 'Cloud

Serpent' and he was associated with lightning, thunder and tempests – his followers saw lightning bolts as the hunter god's darts. He appeared as a deer or rabbit or as a hunter carrying a bundle of arrows. He was also identified as the father of the Feathered Serpent god Quetzalcóatl. In the account of the Toltecs' southward migration from the northern deserts, Mixcóatl was their leader and his son was Topiltzin-Quetzalcóatl the revered ruler of Tollán. In another narrative, Mixcóatl took the form of a deer to chase the fertility and earth goddess Cihuacóatl ('Female Serpent'), and – catching her at last – fathered the Feathered Serpent god.

In the Aztec era, Mixcóatl and fellow hunting god Camaxtli were honoured in Tenochtitlán

Right: This ceramic vessel in the form of a duck is decorated with jade and shells. It was made in Teotihuacán c.AD500.

in the festival of Tóxcatl ('Drought'), when impersonators of these gods and of the dark lord of fate Tezcatlipoca were put to death, and in that of Quecholli ('Treasured Feather'), when hunting contests were held and prisoners of war dressed as deer were sacrificed. The Aztecs also made offerings to Opochtli ('Left-handed'), the god of bird-catchers and fishermen, praising him as the inventor of the nets used for catching birds and the harpoon with which eagle-eyed fishermen speared fish in the waters.

SKILLED IN ANCIENT CRAFTS

The skilled craftsmen and women of the Aztec empire were a discrete class who could claim social status partway between the common folk and the *pipiltin* nobility. Workers such as basketmakers, potters and weavers were the inheritors of ancient Mesoamerican tradition and passed their skills down the generations.

AZTEC ARTISANS

From the time of San José Mogote *c.*1350BC, craftworkers traditionally occupied their own quarters of a settlement. In the Aztec era, most lived in the large cities of the Valley of Mexico, although there were concentrations of artisans in other parts of the Aztec domain.

Below: The intricate patterns of relief brickwork at sites such as Mitla might have been inspired by designs on woven robes.

Right: Scholars believe that traditional weaving in Mexico today follows patterns established in ancient times.

The *amanteca* or feather-workers were based in their own quarter in Tlatelolco, where they elected officials from their number to govern craft business and worshipped their own patron deity in a local temple. The *amanteca* made clothing, dancing costumes, bracelets, banners, magnificent headdresses and ceremonial military items such as shields. Theirs was painstaking work. When they were making feather-decorated clothes, they tied the feathers' stems one at a time into the fabric when weaving. When they were making a banner or a shield, they sewed the feathers individually on to a backing, usually made of paper attached to reeds and covered in leather. They used a

mixture of feathers from local birds and brightly coloured plumage brought by traders from the tropical rainforests of the Maya lowlands. Friar Bernardino de Sahagún describes their craft, adding that the use of tropical feathers was a recent innovation among the Aztecs.

ROBES, BASKETS AND POTS

Weavers made cloth of plant fibres from maguey agave or henequen for the clothes of the common people and spun cotton cloth for the nobility. Women performed the spinning and weaving of the cloth. Cotton was imported into highland Mexico from lowland areas of Mesoamerica. The fineness of the material was the sole difference between the clothes of rich and poor: weavers produced the same range of clothes – loincloths, capes, skirts and large cloaks called *huipiles* – for both nobles and commoners. These often bore embroidered, woven, painted or dyed decorations to signal social class or region of origin.

Like their forebears for thousands of years, Aztec basketmakers made use of the reeds that grew thickly around the lakes of the Valley of Mexico. They also used the leaves of maguey agave, palmleaf and several cacti in their work. They made a wide range of baskets, from compact, tightly woven containers for small valuables to large lidded chests for use as clothes baskets. They also made containers for grain and foodstuffs. The reed craftsmen also made mats and simple stools. Mats

TOOLS AND TOOLMAKERS

For many thousands of years, artisans, soldiers and farmers used tools of obsidian, flint and wood developed in the earliest days of Mesoamerica. Only in the last few centuries of the region's history did its people – notably the Tarascans – begin to make and use metal weapons.

Among the oldest known tools in Mexico is a collection of obsidian scrapers, knives and weapon points, together with some flint blades, made in the region of Lake Texcoco c.7700BC. Prehistoric hunter-gatherers also made cutting tools from the volcanic rock andesite. The first farmers developed the use of a sharpened wooden planting stick. With some improvements, these basic tools remained in use across the millennia. Elite soldiers in the Aztec army were still using weapon points of obsidian in their wooden *atlatl* dart-throwers some 9,000 years later. Generations of Mesoamericans made their livelihood from mining and trading in obsidian, or fashioning it into tools, weapons and other items in workshops.

Metal weapons and tools were not made in Mesoamerica until after c.AD800. The necessary skills were passed along trade routes from South America, probably by sea to western Mexico and overland to the Maya regions of Guatemala, Belize and Mexico. However, it is striking that in western Mexico comparatively few metal tools or weapons were made. Most production was of bells, pins, figurines and jewellery for the elite. The quality of stone and shell tools must have been high enough to prevent their being superseded. In addition to copper, gold and silver were also worked.

Above: This richly coloured painted bowl, probably made for a Maya nobleman or prince, has been dated to c.AD600–900.

were in particularly high demand both for common houses and royal residences, since the Aztecs rarely used furniture.

Potters made a variety of ceramic wares for home cooking and storage, for decorative use by the wealthy and nobility and for ritual use in temples. Without the use of the potter's wheel, they made all their containers and figurines by hand moulding. One favoured method was to build up coils of clay then use a scraping tool to thin out the walls of the pot. Both Aztec and Maya potters produced work of great delicacy and expressiveness.

MAYA CRAFTS

In Maya lands, as in Aztec cities, it was common for craft specialists to live grouped together in a residential area. The craft was probably handed down through the generations, so a craft living unit might also have been a family group. As among the Aztecs, weaving was performed by women. As a spindle they used a thin stick weighted at one end with a ceramic disc. Resting the heavy end on a gourd on the ground, the spinner twirled the spindle to spin the cotton thread. Her companion worked a simple loom on her lap to produce a cloth around 1m (3ft)

wide. The goddess of weaving, Ix Chebal Yax, gave her blessing to this method and was shown using this type of loom in an image in the *Madrid Codex*. The weavers produced different types of cloth and traditional designs in different areas.

Maya basketmakers created containers of intricate and varied weave. None has survived to be examined by archaeologists, but a representation of a basket on Lintel 24 at Yaxchilán shows a complex pattern and indicates the quality of Maya basketwork.

Feather-workers produced a magnificent range of headdress decorations, capes, ceremonial shields and weapons, fans and fringed cloth. They also decorated wicker frames that dancers wore on their backs and protective canopies for royal thrones. In some areas, for instance among the Quiché Maya, birds were bred in captivity for their plumage. Hunters and trackers brought back the feathers of the macaw, the quetzal and other birds from tropical forests. The quetzal was sacred, its feathers symbolic of royal authority.

MASTERS OF THE PAINTED WORD

Scribes were talented, highly educated individuals who combined the skills of painter and writer. In the Aztec empire they were trained in the elite *calmecac* schools at which the children of the nobility and a few precociously talented commoners learned the use of the sacred calendar, the timing of religious festivals, temple rituals, history, astronomy, arithmetic, oratory and the art of *tlacuilloli* or how to 'write-paint'. They were known as *tlacuiloque* or painter-writers. The script they used, which combined pictures that stood for ideas, words and numbers with others that represented a sound from spoken language, was closely derived from ancient Mesoamerican writing systems developed by the Olmec and Zapotecs. It was read in the Aztec tongue Nahuatl, but would have been largely comprehensible to the Maya and to other peoples. This made it highly suitable for keeping records of trade and tribute among the many ethnic and linguistic groups of the empire.

WRITTEN FORMS

The Aztec literate elite produced many different types of book, and scribes probably specialized in one kind. In addition to manuscripts on the ritual calendar and astronomy used for telling fortunes and predicting the future, Aztec scribes made maps, genealogies, histories or annals, law books, tribute lists and documents on dreams. They made ritual

Above: The Maya logograph for 'book', pronounced hun, *represents leaves of bark paper pressed between jaguar-skin covers.*

books or *tonalamatls* and annals or *xiuhamatls* in the form of screenfolds, often from pieces of deerskin stuck together with glue and covered on both sides with white lime. Scribes fashioned some screenfold books from *amatl* paper, produced from the bark of the wild fig tree. They also used *amatl* paper to make long pull-out scrolls or *tiras* and also, one piece at a time, for legal and administrative documents. They painted genealogies and maps on *lienzos*, large pieces of cotton.

KEEPER OF THE BOOKS

Among the Maya of the Classic Period, scribes were treated with great respect as men of genius. Here too, scribes were both writers and artists. Yucatec-speaking Maya called a scribe *ah ts'ib* ('He who Performs Writing and Painting'). From post-conquest accounts, we know that the Maya, like the Aztecs, wrote and kept a wide range of books, including maps, genealogies, medical treatises, books on healing plants, documents about the animals of the wild, as well as priestly

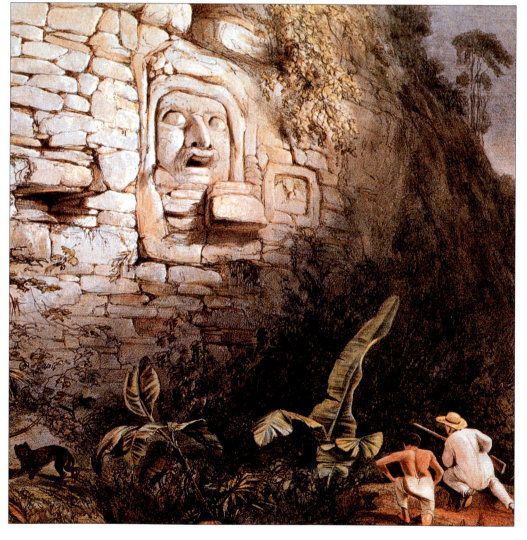

Left: Frederick Catherwood's 19th-century drawing is of a head of Itzamná, inventor of writing, carved in a wall at Izamal, Yucatán.

Left: Aztec scribes wrote the Codex Borbonicus *around the time of the Spanish Conquest to delineate divine influences.*

In representations of high-ranking groups on vases, in murals and in relief carvings, Michael Coe has identified that a batch of sticks worn in the headdress was intended to represent scribal pens and was a sign that the individual either held the position of a scribe or, while occupying another court position, was proud of his ability to read and write. Even kings were depicted with the scribal pens in their headdress.

It is indicative of the high regard for individual scribe-artists and their work among the Maya that the scribes who decorated and wrote on the beautiful ceramic products of the Classic Period signed their names on the pots as they finished them. A city-state's chief scribe appears to have lived in the utmost splendour. At Copán, a magnificent building known to archaeologists as the House of the Bacabs has been identified as the home of Max Chanal, chief scribe in the reign of King Yax Pac (AD763–820).

textbooks on the ritual calendar and the movements of the stars. Unfortunately these books were almost all destroyed in the frenzy of book-burning unleashed by Spanish administrators and churchmen who considered them to be idolatrous.

The scholar Nikolai Grube showed that the highest-ranking Maya scribes were also known as *ah k'u'hun* or *ah k'un* ('Keeper of the Sacred Books') and suggested that they were in charge of the king's library. Fellow Maya expert Michael Coe then demonstrated that the *ah k'un* was a key senior administrator who served as master of ceremonies for state and religious ritual, a marriage negotiator and as the writer of royal genealogies and keeper of tribute lists.

In the Classic Period, Maya scribes were educated in scribal schools close to the palace in the centre of Maya cities. The schools were open to the elite, to the offspring of rulers and the upper nobility. Eldest sons would probably have been destined for military training and power, but younger sons, and probably also sons by less senior wives or concubines, would have entered the schools, happy to take the first steps in the prestigious life of the scribe. Women could also be scribes among the Maya and the schools must have taken princesses and the daughters of the nobility.

LITERARY ELITE

Scribes' work was performed by the elite for the elite. In Classic Period Maya cities, an estimated one-quarter of the population could read and write. A larger number, perhaps, could read inscriptions on stelae without being able to write and many more again could admire the artistic achievement of the *ah ts'ib* while having the meaning of the words explained. Among the elite, it was a matter of great pride to be literate.

Right: This figure of a seated Maya scribe was displayed in one of the houses of the elite quarter of Las Sepulturas in Copán.

A SOLDIER'S LIFE

The attractions of a soldier's life were many. In Aztec society members of the army were respected as paragons of courage and fortitude. They were understood to be fulfilling Tenochtitlán's sacred destiny as an imperial power and to be following divine orders to bring prisoners home for sacrifice. When they died, their souls would travel to the east and be made honourable companions of the great sun Tonatiuh himself. Moreover, the military offered one of the few avenues by which a commoner could climb through the ranks of Aztec society. Success in battle, particularly the capture of many prisoners, won a war hero many coveted privileges, such as the right to wear more elaborate clothes, to partake of the alcoholic drink *pulque* in public or even to join the elite military cadres of the jaguar- and eagle-warriors. These top-ranking figures wore magnificent battle costume to go to war and to take part in ceremonial dances and sacred rituals.

A successful warrior won acclaim and seniority within his own *capultin* or clan. Because he had brought glory on the

Below: The soldiers shown in this mural may be mythical figures representing the forces of night taking on the armies of day.

Above: The Atzecs inherited from the Toltecs the ideal of warriors as embodiments of manly vigour and defenders of divine order.

group, he was awarded extra portions of land, or a larger share of any imperial tribute accorded them. He might be named *tecuhtli* ('Grandfather') and in meetings of the clan council his views were respected.

AZTEC RANK AND FILE

Most soldiers were conscripts called up for a campaign by the military establishment in units of around 400 from each *capultin*, or units in a tribute payment of fighting men supplied to the army of the Triple Alliance by one of the empire's subject cities. They would have had a good military training as part of their education in the *telpochcalli* school attached to the local temple. Many also took part in ceremonial military activities as part of religious festivals. Where possible, inexperienced men fought behind veteran warriors. Sometimes novice fighters wore no protective armour, as the wearing of quilted cotton body armour was often restricted to warriors who had achieved glory by killing or capturing many victims. Clan group members wore tribal symbols.

INJURED IN BATTLE

Most Aztec battles were over swiftly, with prisoners of war often far outnumbering battlefield casualties and fatalities. Nevertheless, Mesoamerican armies contained skilled doctors, who accompanied soldiers on campaign equipped with herbs and other natural materials and a wealth of traditional medical knowledge. Army surgeons used obsidian knives to make surgical cuts and human hair to sew up wounds. They even made plaster from tree sap and feathers to set broken bones.

When a soldier was injured by a sharp obsidian *atlatl* dart, the doctor would first clean the wound with whatever sterile liquid was available – if necessary, by using his own urine. Afterwards he looked in his medical bag for a little of the herb he called *coapatli* (a wild form of the common dayflower) to stop the soldier's bleeding. The sap of the maguey agave, which when fermented made the favoured drink *pulque*, was an effective dressing. The doctor gave a herbal painkiller to soldiers who were in terrible pain.

ESCAPING ONE'S ORIGINS

Among the Maya, those who won status as warriors rose from the mass of farmer-commoners to a position halfway up the social pyramid, on a level with artisans and administrators. As among the Aztecs, successful warriors were rewarded with social prestige. Any killed in battle would receive preferential treatment in the after-life, for they were earmarked – along with sacrificial victims, priests, rulers, those who died giving birth and those who hung themselves – for a heavenly place of rest, while the unhappy majority of humankind went down to the dark place of trials, Xibalba. Maya rank and file

Below: Wielding spears, Maya warriors sweep resistance aside as they capture a village in Yucatán.

soldiers fought in cotton jerkins or simple loincloths and cloaks, while nobles and elite warriors wore feather-bedecked helmets and jade jewellery. The king went to battle magnificently attired in a jaguar tunic, a symbol of royalty and of ferocious martial strength. He must have been more of a figurehead than a combatant

Above: A detail from the Mixtec Codex Zouche-Nuttall *depicts warrior leaders crossing a river in order to take an island.*

and was protected by a group of elite fighters. The capture of a king was a tremendous coup and ended any battle. In Aztec and Maya realms, the warrior was an ideal, a role occupied or assumed by the ruler. The images of kings carved on the stelae erected in Maya cities from the late Preclassic Period onwards presented the king as warrior and priestly sacrificer, imbued with divine power. The king received this power from his predecessor and passed it on to his successor. He was the link – like the great ceiba tree – between the terrestrial plane of daily life and the heavenly realm of the ancestors.

Martial vigour and achievement was seen as proof of the king's stature and status. Newly elected Aztec *tlatoanis* were required to conduct a war as part of their extended coronation rites; the king of a Classic Period Maya city often undertook a military raid in order to obtain victims to be sacrificed as part of the king's own coronation ceremony. Shield Jaguar II of Yaxchilán took a notable local lord, Ah Ahau, captive in a raid of AD680 that scholars believe was a prelude to Shield Jaguar II's coronation the following year.

IN THE STATE'S SERVICE

The administration of the Aztec empire and its largely self-governing constituent units was a major task and provided employment for large numbers or people. All the most important and senior positions were filled by members of the *pipiltin* nobility. Nobles served as advisers to the ruler, as ambassadors, as governors of allied provinces, as judges, as collectors of tax and tribute, as leading members of the military hierarchy and as bureaucrats. Others joined the priesthood, where they had opportunities to pursue intellectual interests in, say, astronomy, mathematics or writing. All these men were graduates of elite *calmecac* priestly schools.

Commoners – whose living came from farming, fishing, hunting, soldiering, artisan work or mercantile activity – could rise to positions of authority within the *capultin* or tribal clans to which they

Below: A painted Maya pot of c.AD600–900, from the Motagua valley, shows a dignitary carrying shield and spear.

belonged. One was elected *calpullec*, who oversaw economic matters, such as grants of land, within the clan; another was the *teochcautin*, the keeper of laws. At times of conflict, the *teochcautin* led the clan's conscripts to war.

THE KING'S MEN

Similarly, in Maya culture commoner-farmers, fishermen and soldiers could not rise to the most senior administrative and economic positions. In the Maya cities of the Classic Period, the top military staff, administrators and traders were all members of the upper nobility. The top military chief, *sahal*, was generally one of the king's closest relatives.

In Postclassic Yucatán, as described by Bishop Diego de Landa, the ruler of a regional state, called the *halach uinic*, appointed those who governed the towns

Above: Clay figurines from Jaina Island show the elaborate headdresses, jewellery and other adornments of the Maya elite.

and villages of the region from the highest levels of royalty and the nobility, including his own nephews, cousins and brothers. Each of these men, who were called *batabs*, ruled through a council of two or three and decisions on regional matters had to be approved unanimously by all councillors.

The *batab* was the local judge and military leader. He ensured that his town or region was ready with its economic tribute when required by the *halach uinic*. The *batab* had two or three deputies called *ah kulelob* to perform his bidding. He worked closely with a military specialist called a *nacom*, a noble who served in this highly prestigious and coveted position for three years. During this period, he was required to live a celibate and sober life, with no contact of any kind with women. Even those who waited upon him and served his food were required to be men.

Another group of senior administrators were the *ah holpopob* who ran the council meeting house and were well informed on matters of foreign interaction. Day-to-day matters such as village disputes or petty crimes were the province of the *tupiles* or local law officers.

COPÁN'S GOVERNORS

Archaeologists working at Copán have uncovered details of civil administrators in the reign of King Yax Pac (AD763–820). Leading nobles, who lived in the region of Copán called Las Sepulturas by historians, were members of Copán's ruling council and each headed a prestigious blood lineage. Their houses have been excavated and contain splendid carved benches that suggest that these men had significant independent authority and wealth.

One of these was the king's chief scribe, Max Chanal, whose house contains several portraits of him holding his tools. A delicately carved bench dedicated in AD781 celebrates his own rank, his proud descent and the might of his king.

Yax Pac's brothers, Yahua Chan and Yax K'amlay, were also important figures in the administration. Scholars believe that the king's authority was failing and that he attempted to bolster it by giving more power to his brothers and to leading nobles. However, the attempt was doomed to failure. After his death, the dynasty and Copán itself suffered the effects of a decline that had already begun some years earlier.

Above: This pectoral or chest piece is made from jade and comes from Nebaj, Guatemala, c.AD300–900. It depicts a seated nobleman.

THE QUICHÉ ARISTOCRACY

Among the Quiché Maya of highland Guatemala, once again, commoners were excluded from the highest levels of government and administration. The nobility or *ahauab* were descendants of the Quiché founders, who were probably originally Putún Maya merchants from the Gulf Coast lowlands of Mexico. The *ahauab* provided rulers, military leaders, priests and administrators.

Members of the middle class could find work as land managers, soldiers, traders and bureaucrats. The *ahauab* were organized into groups depending on descent from a common father. Members of particular kin groups specialized in serving as priests, warriors or administrators. The leaders of these kin groups governed their relatives and served as advisers to the Quiché ruler.

At the Quiché capital Utatlan in the 15th century, three lineages were pre-eminent and identified with gods: the Ahau Quiché were followers of the sky god, the Nihaib were dependents of the moon goddess and the Cawek were devotees of the sun god. Their elite members filled the top administrative posts of army captain, judge and other positions identified as 'speaker' and 'receiving officer', a kind of ambassador and master of ceremonies who received important visitors. Above them all was the ahpop ('Ruler or Mat Lord'). He was high priest, army leader and chairman of the ruling council.

Below: A limestone carving from Palenque shows King Pacal, seated on a regal jaguar-head stool, receiving a headdress – and so divine authority to rule – from his mother Zac Kuk. Archaeologists found the relief inside House E of the Palenque palace.

NOBLE SERVANTS OF THE GODS

In Maya lands, entering the priesthood was not generally an option for the sons of farmers, artisans or merchants: the most important priestly positions – like the top administrative and legal opportunities – were hereditary and passed down the generations by members of the nobility. Bishop Diego de Landa reported that in the 16th century the leading Maya priests trained their own sons or the younger boys of important lords, while the high priest was succeeded by his son or nearest blood relative.

SERVANTS OF THE SUN

De Landa wrote that the high priest was called *ahuacan* ('Lord Snake') and was kept in fine style by gifts and contributions from secular rulers. He was the final authority on arcane priestly matters concerning astronomy, divination, writing and record keeping, interpreting holy books, the setting of festivals and the ritual to be followed. He led sacrifices and ritual worship only on very important occasions and also oversaw the training and appointment of more junior priests.

The word for priest was *ah kin* ('Servant of the Sun'). One was appointed to discover and interpret the prophecies associated with each of the 13 *katuns* – periods of 7,200 days – that recurred in a cycle as part of the Maya Long Count. Other leading Maya priests at the time of Bishop de Landa were the *chilanes* ('Declaimers'), who functioned as oracles, passing on to eager listeners the decrees and warnings of the gods. These men were shaman-diviners, who reported on the reality they discovered during spirit voyages or in the course of religious visions inspired by mind-altering drugs.

Another priest was the *nacom*, who was entrusted with the crucial sacrificial task of slicing open the victim's chest and removing the heart. This skilled executioner's position was held by a man for his lifetime. His four helpers, who held down the writhing body of the victim on the sacrificial stone, were named *chacs* in honour of the rain god. They also had the task of lighting a new sacred fire at the beginning of each year.

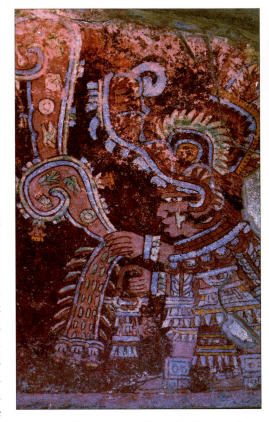

Above: A fresco image from the Tepantitla apartment building in Teotihuacán depicts a priest making obeisance to the deities.

These roles certainly had their counterparts in Maya cities of the Classic Period, although the details of sacrificial practice and priestly hierarchy probably differed. From the very beginnings of settled life in Maya lands, it appears that priests specialized in knowledge of astronomic cycles and seasonal change. They became specialists in time, maintaining control over the recurring patterns of religious life by setting dates for festivals and becoming repositories of dynastic history. They developed the elite skills of writing and reading and, by the Classic Period, were closely associated, if not synonymous, with the scribes and stonemasons who were so revered for their written art.

Left: Wearing facepaint, elaborate costumes and headgear and carrying ritual staffs, Mixtec priests advance to sacrifice.

TEMPLE WOMEN

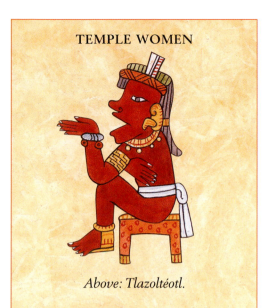

Above: Tlazoltéotl.

There were many opportunities for women in Aztec religious life. The major goddesses were served by cadres of female priests. For example, priestesses of the fertility goddess Tlazoltéotl heard confessions from those wishing to own up to sexual wrongdoing. The priestess of Chalchiúhtlicue, goddess of rivers and ocean, performed a rite of blessing for newborn babies, sprinkling the infant with holy water. Priestesses also represented and impersonated their patron during religious festivals. During the festival of Huey Tozoztli ('Major Vigil'), the priestess of corn goddess Chicomecóatl pronounced a blessing over farmers' supply of seeds.

In Ochpaniztli ('Clearing'), the harvest celebration, the Chicomecóatl priestess sacrificed and flayed a female victim and donned her skin as a suit. With another priestess, appearing as the fertility goddess Toci, she then hurled fistfuls of corn into the crowd. Farmers kept the seeds for planting next season.

Some priestesses, the *maqui*, served as temple prostitutes. They were visited by young warriors, travelled with the army on campaign and even marched into battle. Their divine patron was Xochiquetzal, goddess of flowers.

Above: The goggle eyes of the rain god can be seen on this ceramic figurine of a splendidly attired priest from Teotihuacán.

MANY PRIESTS, MANY TASKS

While the top-level priests were all members of the *pipiltin* nobility in Aztec society, members of any class could become rank and file priests. There was a range of opportunities for priests. Top-level sacerdotal administrators supervised the ranks of priests, the priestly schools, the performance of ritual and the practical management of temple finances and landholdings. Elite serving priests led worship in the Templo Major and main temples and performed major sacrifices on important religious feast days. Other sons of the nobility lived as monk-like attendants and celebrants in the great temples. Each painted his body black or wore a long, black-hooded cloak. They were celibate and often fasted for festivals. Their hair was matted with blood from the cuts they made to their head during rites of autosacrifice.

Right: The elaborate ritual costume, headgear and jewellery worn by Maya priests are depicted in delicate detail on a stela from the mid-8th century AD.

Some priests were members of the army and marched into battle alongside high-ranking soldiers in the centre of the army's battle line. They carried images of Huitzilopochtli and other deities. Others worked in *calmecac* schools, where all the teachers were priests. Some were the learned artist-scribes who expressed their vast knowledge of astronomical cycles and ritual worship in codex books. Others were shaman-diviners, gifted with spiritual vision, the capacity to interpret it and the gift of spirit and body healing.

CHAPTER FIVE

EVERYDAY LIFE

The day started early for Mesoamericans: the people of Tenochtitlán rose before dawn. When the morning star, Venus, appeared in the sky, drums and conch trumpets sounded from the Templo Mayor and the temples that were the focus of religious life in each locality. The *tlatoani*, his relatives and the nobles, priests, farmers, fishermen, hunters and merchants all awoke. Many took a steam bath to refresh themselves. For most, breakfast was a few tortillas or tamales, perhaps a cup of *atolli* or maize soup. Labourers carried a few more maize snacks to work for a midday meal.

In a Maya village or city of the Classic Period, the first hours of the day were markedly similar. The majority rose before dawn, took a steam bath, ate a maize breakfast and made their way to the fields, artisan-workshop or other place of work grasping a few tortillas for later sustenance.

After a long day's labour, most workers were home before dark. They ate their largest meal, again based on maize, at this time. Some accounts suggest that labourers, hungry from their labours in the fields, ate as many as 20 large tortillas at evening meal. Men and women usually ate separately, squatting or sitting on the floor. Afterwards, lighting their homes with pine torches, both men and women often settled down to craft-work, perhaps chipping simple tools from flint or making pots for their own use. Merchants, by contrast, sometimes hosted elaborate feasts, while in noble houses evenings of poetry and music might be laid on in gardens and patio areas giving on to luxuriously appointed dining areas.

Left: A page from the Mixtec Codex Zouche-Nuttall *depicts the wedding of Lady 3-Flint to Lord 12-Wind.*

LIFE IN THE HOME

In Tenochtitlán, the *tlatoani's* divine magnificence was reflected in the splendour of his elegantly decorated palace, surrounded by gardens containing ponds, walkways, an aviary and even a zoo. Members of the *pipiltin* nobility also had palatial residences with a *temazcalli* or steam bath and expansive gardens, while wealthy merchants and craftsmen expressed their social standing in fine, but much smaller houses. The home of a common family was a single-roomed hut, or a few rooms clustered around a courtyard. Walls were usually of adobe or wattle and daub, although some wealthier commoners lived in stone buildings.

Multiroom houses contained one or more bedrooms, a living room with a central hearth and perhaps a bathroom. Single-room huts provided little more

Below: Aztecs lived on or near the floor, sitting on reed mats to eat and work at weaving or toolmaking close to the hearth.

Above: This modern reconstruction of an Aztec working family shows a farmer bringing home crops while his relatives weave and attend to the children.

than a space for sleeping, with the family hearth often situated outside beneath a canopy. The family might keep a turkey or a small dog in a pen alongside the house or a few birds in a cage. Many households also had a small garden called a *xochichinancalli* ('flowerbed among the reeds') for growing vegetables, flowers and healing herbs. All houses had a shrine to the ancestors. The location as well as the size of a family's home depended on their wealth and social standing.

WORKING FROM HOME

Home was a place of labour for women, who spent long hours spinning, weaving and cooking. They span thread from maguey agave, henepen or cotton using a handheld drop spindle, working it into woven cloth using a loom strapped on the back and held in the lap. When not weaving or sewing, they ground maize for hours using a rolling stone or pestle at a low table called a *metatl*. With maize dough they made tortillas on a large clay disc laid over a fire on three hearthstones.

Poorer families generally lived farther away from the city centre. They often lived in single-room huts, whereas the better off families lived in stone buildings nearer the city's ceremonial precincts and major markets. Aztec houses had little or no furniture: people worked, sat and ate on the floor. They usually slept on woven reed mats.

The men worked in the *chinampa* fields or took their boats, nets and harpoons out fishing on the lake. They taught their sons how to fish and encouraged them to try their luck at catching birds. If the conscription call came, they could be forced to go on military campaign in the army or perhaps to serve as labourers in a vast building construction project designed to express the might and celebrate the religious devotion of the 'people of the sun'.

Left: The kind of thatched hut typically occupied by Maya peasants is depicted amid trees in a detail from a temple mural.

WITHIN THE CORNER POSTS

In the lowlands of the central Maya region, the typical commoner's house was built on a low platform of earth or rubble, with walls of stone, mud blocks or adobe built around four wooden corner posts and a roof of pole and thatch. Sometimes only the lower half of the wall was made of long-lasting materials such as stone or adobe, and the upper part was filled in with straw or reeds. The house contained one or two rooms at most.

Builders often laid out three or four of these small constructions around a central courtyard. According to Bishop Diego de Landa, the Maya of Yucatán split these houses lengthways by building an internal wall. In the rear, private part they built bed frames of branches and saplings over which they laid mats as mattresses. Here they slept, using cloaks as coverings.

The front part of the house functioned as a kind of porch, and provided a cooler place to sleep in hot weather. In some areas a family group might have used several small buildings arranged around a central yard: one for storing food, tools and equipment, one for sleeping, one as a living area, one as a shrine, one as a workshop for making stone tools – and a small hut with a central fire heating stones for use as a steam room. Some Maya villagers stored food and water in pits called *chultunes* dug in the ground.

As among the Aztecs, the majority of men were away from home for long hours working in the fields or hunting. At home, the women worked ceaselessly spinning, weaving, grinding flour, preparing food, tending to the garden and the needs of the turkeys or dogs they kept for meat.

Any cloth that was not needed, together with surplus vegetables or other items that could be spared from the garden were taken to the nearest market to be sold or to barter for items which the family did not make themselves.

At times of sowing and harvest the division of labour shifted, so that women went out to assist their menfolk in the fields with the extra seasonal work.

FAMILY NETWORK

People tended to live in family or extended family groups. At Tikal, an extended family often lived in houses arranged on the north, south and west sides of a courtyard and facing east towards a fourth building on a higher platform. This probably contained a shrine to the ancestors and, beneath the floor, the graves of the most revered among past family members.

All members of Maya settlements lived in the same pattern of buildings. Wealthier members such as nobles, traders, military leaders and the king lived in increasingly splendid versions of the basic buildings.

Below: Carving on an archway in Labná depicts a simple, one-roomed thatched hut.

THE MATCHMAKER'S ART

Among the Maya of Yucatán at the time of the Spanish Conquest, girls and boys who reached puberty went through a ceremony named the Descent of the Gods. The sacred rite, performed by a priest with the help of local elders, set the young apart from their childhood. From that day onwards, they were considered to be members of the adult community.

Girls were then judged to be ready for marriage. Their mothers taught them the skills necessary for married life and instructed their daughters in modesty. This included showing her how, when she met a man on a path, she should turn away and present her back to him, so that he could pass easily and undisturbed. The young woman was also instructed that, if she came to the well with her cousin or another man, she should keep her eyes gently lowered as she brought him water.

In some Maya communities, sons left the parental house and moved into a communal building set aside for unmarried men. There they played dice and games with small balls and beans. It was not unknown for these young men to bring prostitutes home and they paid for their services with a handful of cacao beans. Unmarried men marked themselves out by painting their skin with black dye. They avoided tattoos, which were only permitted to husbands.

MARRIAGE PLANNING

Marriages were generally arranged, either by the father or by a professional matchmaker called an *ah atanzah*. The ideal wife would be a woman of the same social level and from the same village as the son. Marriage plans were often agreed between families while the son and daughter to be wed were still children; the families then began to live as in-laws even though the marriage might be some years off.

Before any marriage agreement was made, both families consulted the priestly astronomers who made sure that there was no ill omen attached to the prospective couple's dates of birth or to the day proposed for the wedding ceremony. Marriages were permitted between first cousins, but some unions were taboo. For example, a man could not marry a woman who carried the same surname or patronym.

Left: Xochiquetzal, ('Precious Flower') was honoured by the Aztecs as a goddess of love, domesticity and the flowers of the earth.

Above: Chalchiúhtlicue, who presided over the prolonged wedding ceremonies of the Aztecs, is usually shown wearing jade.

The marriage ceremony was held in the house of the bride's father. The couple wore new robes woven for the occasion by the two mothers. After the wedding the new husband and wife lived in the house or the group of houses occupied by the bride's family for about six or seven years. The husband's new in-laws benefited from his labour throughout this time and, indeed, by custom could evict him from their home compound if he refused to work.

After this the couple moved to live adjacent to the husband's father, often in a newly built house within the complex. Commoners had one wife, but wealthier men could wed several women. Members of the elite in Classic Period Maya cities such as Tikal took many wives and also kept women outside wedlock as concubines.

DEATH AND DIVORCE

A couple could divorce simply by one partner repudiating the other. Younger children of the wedding would remain with the mother, while older children tended to go with the same-sex parent.

Left: A scene from the Codex Becker *shows the wedding of a Mixtec noble couple. Faint footsteps lead to their future offspring.*

A man might divorce his wife if she proved unable to have children or if she failed in duties such as making food or preparing his evening bath. Any remarriage took place without ceremony, as wedding rites were reserved for first marriages. A man seeking a new union would simply visit the house of the woman he had chosen. If she was agreeable she would prepare him a meal. Widows and widowers were expected to mourn the lost partner for a year before remarrying. A widower could not marry his dead wife's sister or mother.

CHALCHIÚHTLICUE'S BLESSING

Customs were not very different among the Aztecs. Weddings came under the protection of river and ocean goddess Chalchiúhtlicue. Young Aztecs married in their late teenage years or perhaps their early twenties. The young man's parents arranged his marriage after consulting with members of the extended family or kin group. They sent a professional matchmaker to the parents of the chosen young woman. The matchmaker presented his case on four consecutive days, after which the parents of the young woman were expected to announce whether they accepted the marriage offer or not.

The marriage ceremony lasted four days. On the evening of the first day, the bride was bathed and dressed in fine robes, before her kinswomen decorated her legs and arms with red feathers and painted her face with a paste containing tiny, shimmering crystals. They offered

her words of wisdom about the life she was preparing to begin, then the strongest one lifted the bride on to her back and carried her through the streets to the house of the husband's parents.

Inside, amid scenes of celebration, the couple sat side by side on a marriage mat, while elders lit a fire in the family hearth and burned offerings of copal incense, which sent up sacred clouds of smoke to attract the gods' blessings. The groom's mother produced a wealth of robes and mantles as gifts for her prospective in-laws. Then a matchmaker approached the couple and tied the groom's cape to the bride's skirt and the groom's mother fed first the bride and then the groom with

four mouthfuls of tamales, a dish prepared of meat and corn husks. This ceremony marked the couple's union: next they were led into the bedroom to consummate their marriage, while the gathered relatives made merry.

Feasting continued for four days. At the end of this time, a series of formal speeches concluded the celebration. First, the most respected elder female on the new husband's side reminded the new wife of her duties and of the need to be trusting, humble and hard working. The mother of the bride spoke next, to her new son-in-law, asking him to remember that he owed his wife a duty of love, hard work and self-sacrificing attention.

Below: The bride arrives at her wedding on the back of her matchmaker (bottom centre) and is shown, later, seated on a mat.

A CHILD IS BORN

When a pregnant woman went into labour, her midwife would lead prayers to the goddess of childbirth – Tlazoltéotl among the Aztecs and Ix Chel among the Maya – to ease the woman's pain and bring a healthy baby. The midwife mixed herbs and grasses to produce a sedative mixture that she fed to the mother. She then gently laid a warm stone on her straining belly. Among the Aztecs, when the baby was born the midwife would utter a series of battle cries in praise of the exhausted mother who had fought long and hard with her offspring in

labour. Then the midwife would speak to the baby, greeting the new arrival as if it were a voyager who had completed a long and difficult journey, encouraging the infant to settle among its family, declaring that life in the world was short but a man or woman had many duties, the most important of which were to work hard and to honour the gods.

The midwife would next cut the baby's umbilical cord and store it safely, before giving the baby its first bath, explaining in a reverent voice that pure and cleansing waters were the gift of Chalchiúhtlicue, the consort of Tláloc the rain god and goddess of springs, rivers and the sea. If the baby were a boy, he was expected to keep the umbilical cord until adulthood and carry it to a distant battlefield, where it was his duty to bury it; a girl would bury her umbilical cord beside the family hearth.

Left: Heavy with the power of fertility, this statue of a pregnant woman was made in Nayarit, West Mexico, c.200BC–AD200.

Above: Power over the beginnings of life. This almost abstract face is believed to be that of the Huastec goddess of childbirth.

After its first bath, the newborn was ready to receive visitors. Many members of the extended family came to pay their respects. One after another, they would make reverent declarations of respect for

A NOBLE WELCOMING

Among noble and wealthy Aztecs, a baby's arrival was celebrated with a lying-in that lasted up to three weeks. Visitors came from great distances – some important families even received ambassadors from foreign states. The hosts provided splendid gifts of the finest woven cloaks and embroidered skirts for their prominent guests. Food, *pulque* and other drinks were provided for all who came to pay their respects.

the mother, the midwife and the newborn baby. Visitors were greeted with food and drink. Priestly interpreters of the *tonalamatl* book of the sacred calendar would arrive to interpret the ramifications of the baby's precise minute, hour and day of birth for its prospects and future behaviour.

Much depended on which gods were influential at the child's birth. If the omens were bad, the interpreters offered advice as to how parents and baby could improve the infant's prospects. They also set the date for the baby's bathing ritual: this would normally be four days after the birth, but could be delayed or brought forward if the divine influences on that day were not good.

A BATHING CEREMONY

On the appointed day, the midwife conducted the bathing ceremony in the presence of parents and extended family. She laid a basin of water on a reed mat and surrounded it with miniature tools appropriate to the baby's sex and the family's standing and profession. If a boy child had been destined for the army by the *tonalamatl* priests, the midwife would lay out a small bow and arrow on top of an amaranth-dough tortilla intended to represent a warrior's shield. If he were the son of an artisan, then she would lay out tiny implements representing the father's profession, the path that lay before the boy as he grew. For a female baby, the midwife would place a tiny skirt together with spinning instruments to represent a woman's work.

The midwife then circled the basin in an anticlockwise direction as she spoke to the baby, before she bathed him or her and presented him or her four times to the heavens and to the cleansing water provided by blessed Chalchiúhtlicue. Any older children in the family were next sent out into the street to publicly announce the name chosen for the newborn. The baby was dried, dressed and laid in its cradle while the joyful mother, the father and the assembled relatives celebrated the birth with feasting and music.

Left: The young boy represented by this terracotta statuette, made in Veracruz c.AD550–850, learned to wear headdress, earrings and necklace before clothes.

A WEB OF DIVINE INFLUENCES

The Maya keenly believed the minute, hour and day of a baby's birth in the ritual calendar set the child's temperament, determined its prospects and brought with it religious and ritual responsibilities – acts that were necessary to limit or bring to fruition the divine influences at work in the moment of birth.

Among the Cakchiquel and other southern highland Maya, babies were given the name of the day in the 260-day calendar on which they were born. Among the Yucatec-speaking Maya at the time of the Spanish Conquest, each baby took four names: a name chosen by a priest following a divining ceremony; the father's family name; the family names of father and mother together; and lastly a familiar or nickname.

So developed was the shared aesthetic sense among the Maya that mothers and fathers were willing to work on the baby's body to make it conform to common ideals of beauty. To produce the flattened forehead that was widely admired they bound the baby's head between flat pieces of wood, one pressed against the forehead and one against the back of the skull. After several days encased in this way, a baby's skull was flattened for the remainder of life. The Maya also admired a cross-eyed look, so a mother would tied resin balls to the hairs that fell down towards the eyes of the growing baby to encourage the child to focus on the resin balls.

THE FIRST YEARS

Aztec parents brought their children up to be hardworking, dutiful and self-disciplined. As toddlers grew older, their parents taught them various domestic tasks. At around the age of three, daughters were taught by their mothers to spin and weave, to grind maize and to make tortillas. At the same age, boys began to help around the house, for example, by fetching and carrying water. When boys reached the age of six or seven years, they began to spend their days with their fathers at the lakeside, learning to fish and to gather reeds. If the family made their living by a specialized craft such as pottery or basketmaking, the mother or father would begin instruction in its techniques when the child was aged eight to ten years.

The Aztecs were not averse to using corporal punishment to bring their children into line, although codex accounts suggest that they avoided doing so until the child was around eight or nine years old. The Codex Mendoza shows parents punishing backsliding or lazy children by pinching them on the ears or arms, pricking their skin with the thorns of the maguey cactus, spanking them or binding them up and laying them in a cold, damp place. The most unusual punishment depicted was forcing a child to inhale the burning odours of roasting chilli peppers by holding him or her over a fire on which chillies had been scattered.

AZTEC SCHOOLS

Children progressed to school when they came of age. Scholars are uncertain whether this was at 7, 10 or 14 years. Children of commoners went to the *telpochcalli* ('young person's house') that stood beside their local temple. In sizeable cities there was a *telpochcalli* for each *calpulli* or residential ward. Girls and boys were taught separately. They learned history, public speaking, dancing and singing and received religious instruction. Boys also underwent rigorous military training, while girls learned to serve in the temples of the city. An Aztec education emphasized a young person's duties and responsibilities: he or she was encouraged to find fulfilment in serving the gods, the state, the *calpulli* and the family livelihood.

Sons and daughters of the nobility were educated separately from commoners, in establishments called *calmecac*. They received instruction in religious ritual, in following the sacred calendar and

Left: The Codex Mendoza *shows discipline of 7–10-year-olds. At 7, a boy is taught to fish while a girl learns to spin; beneath, the children are threatened with maguey spikes at age 8, then pricked with the spikes at 9, and bound and beaten at the age of 10.*

Above: The Codex Mendoza *depicts 11-year-olds being forced to inhale chilli smoke; at 13, the boy transports rushes by canoe while the girl grinds maize for tortillas.*

interpreting the *tonalamatl* and in understanding and conducting the main festivals of the Aztec religious year. They also learned military theory, agriculture and horticulture, astronomy, history and the skills of architecture and arithmetic. Students at *calmecac* were also taught and practised the skills of high oratory and of reading and writing. They graduated to become such leading figures of state as judges, military commanders, bureaucrats and priests in the most important temples. A few very able children of commoners were also selected to enjoy the benefits of this elite form of education. There was one elite school for girls and one for boys in each city. Students were expected to follow religious fasts, to perform penances and to take purifying sacred baths. Their teachers were priests.

LEARNING IN MAYA LANDS

The Maya of the Classic Period ran similar elite schools to train the younger sons of royalty and the highest echelons of the nobility as artist-scribes. Some elite Maya scribes were women, so these elite schools must either have accepted female pupils or have operated sister establishments for princesses and the daughters of the nobility.

Less privileged Maya were educated at home in the skills of domestic living and of the family livelihood. For the first three years both boys and girls spent their time almost exclusively with their mother, but from the age of four or five years they began a wider life. At this stage a boy would have a white bead tied in his hair as a sign that he was ready to accompany and begin learning from his father, while a girl had a red shell tied to a string around her waist. Boys went with their fathers to the fields and on hunting trips, day by day picking up the skills they would need in adult life.

*Below: A potter in Tlatilco, Mexico, made this striking and well proportioned ceramic child's head c.400*BC.

95

THE GIFT OF THE MAIZE GOD

Throughout Mesoamerica the staple food was maize. Its preparation was laborious: first it was soaked with lime or ash, then boiled until its skin could be pulled off; afterwards it was ground to a paste with a grooved rolling stone on a long flat stone the Aztecs called a *metatl*. This dough was baked as tortillas (flat, thin cakes) on a circular clay dish supported over the fire by three hearthstones. Maize was cooked with chilli pepper and honey in a soup-like stew the Aztecs called *atolli* and in tamales – mixed with peppers and vegetables or sometimes meat, then wrapped in corn-husks and baked on the cooking plate.

Below: A ceramic Zapotec funerary urn from a Monte Albán tomb depicts the corn god with an animal-mask headdress.

A Maya villager woke to a breakfast of maize water, then left for the fields carrying several balls of ground maize encased in leaves. At night, refreshed after his agricultural labours by a steam bath, he was served tortillas. In Atzec lands a peasant's midday meal consisted of the maize soup *atolli* and his reward for his work in the evening was to dine on tortillas topped with beans, other vegetables and chilli sauce.

FEASTING ON FLESH

Richer members of the Aztec community ate a more elaborate diet, but it was always based on tortillas and tamales. Successful merchants laid on magnificent feasts for their fellows to boost their professional standing. During the festival of Panquetzalíztli, held in honour of the Aztecs' tribal lord Huitzilopochtli, these feasts included the flesh of slaves provided by the merchants to be sacrificed at the temple – served with tortillas, tamales and other maize and bean delicacies. According to the records of the Spanish churchman Bernardino de Sahagún, the *tlatoani* or ruler of Tenochtitlán faced an array of 2,000 dishes every day. This combined basic and luxury foods – tortillas, tamales, turkey, venison, quail, rabbit, hare, rat and many fishes, plus fruits in great variety.

VEGETABLE VARIETY

To supplement their maize, Mesoamericans grew the grain amaranth, called *huautli* in the Aztecs' Nahuatl language. The Aztecs ate a wide range of vegetables including many types of bean, squashes, onions, sweet potatoes (called *camotli*) and a root vegetable

Above: The Tudela Codex *(1553) shows a woman pouring chocolate from a height to give the drink a frothy head.*

called *jicama*, which resembled the turnip. It was added to vegetable stews, steamed or thinly sliced and eaten raw with a spicy chilli and salt seasoning. They also added peanuts and popcorn to their diet. Among fruits they ate the green tomato (called *tomatl*) and the red tomato (*xictomatl*), the avocado (*ahuacatl*), the custard apple, the zapote, the guava and the chirimoya.

The poor ate whatever meat and fish they could add to their diet. The Maya ate deer, home-raised and wild turkeys, iguanas, armadillos, rabbits, peccaries (a pig-like mammal), squirrels, porcupines, monkeys, macaws and other birds and rodents including agouti, paca and doubt-less rats. Those among the Maya who lived in coastal, riverside and lakeside areas ate fish and shellfish while others

Above: On a painted plate from the region of Tikal, an enthroned ruler is being served a cup of the chocolate drink.

made do with dried fish transported by traders. In Tenochtitlán and other Aztec cities, the menfolk caught fish and birds, and they probably hunted rabbits and deer in the countryside. Families raised turkeys and dogs in small pens and birds in cages if they could afford to do so. Sometimes the women-folk traded home-woven cloth and flint tools or obsidian blades made at home by their husbands for deer or rabbit meat at the market.

SEASONINGS AND DRINKS

As well as chilli peppers, Mesoamericans used coriander, sage and the herb dogweed (*chenopodium*) for seasoning. Among other flavourings, they prized vanilla very highly, finding it in the pods of a species of orchid.

The wealthy greatly enjoyed the chocolate drink the Aztecs called *xocolatl*. A man making the drink would grind roasted cacao beans then sometimes mix the powder with dried corn. He would add cold water and beat the liquid until it foamed, then add pods of the vanilla orchid or spoonfuls of honey. The Maya also used a flower called the ear flower (identified by scholars as *Cymbalopetalum penduliflora*) as a flavouring for chocolate drink. In carved and ceramic representations of elite groups, one noble figure is often depicted holding a bundle of these ear flowers.

Xocolatl was a drink of rulers, princes and nobles: some sources suggest that Moctezuma II and his court consumed 50 jugs of the drink every day. The Maya served it in tall cylindrical vases from which they poured it into shallow calabash drinking cups from a great height to generate froth. In AD749, a king of Piedras Negras celebrated the 20th anniversary of his accession with a chocolate-drinking ceremony with leading members of the nobility and an ambassador from Yaxchilán. The event was commemorated in a carved wall panel. Chocolate was also drunk by Maya parents and matchmakers during elite marriage negotiations and it was served at high-class weddings.

Throughout Mesoamerica, people drank an alcoholic drink made from the fermented sap of the maguey agave together with a bush root called pulque wood. The drink was called *pulque* by the Aztecs. They celebrated the goddess Mayáhuel as the divine patron of the drink.

In Aztec lands, *pulque* was officially allowed only to nobles, the ill and the elderly and to warriors brave in battle. There were fierce laws against public drunkenness, enforceable by the death penalty if a person were discovered drunk three times.

Bishop Diego de Landa, describing religious ceremonies celebrated each month by the Maya, suggests that public drinking and intoxication was part of religious ceremonial. Celebrants indulged in a sacred wine called *balche* made from the bark of the balche tree together with water and fermented honey. It was left to steep for some time, during which a prayer was intoned to the spirits of all animals and plants in the surrounding wilderness. It was said to induce feelings of tribal unity and togetherness.

Right: A Huastec statue celebrates corn goddess Chicomecóatl. She was also known as Chicomolotzin ('Seven Ears of Maize').

CLOTHES AND HAIRSTYLES

In Maya lands, commoners, nobility and royalty all wore the same basic clothing but wealthier people possessed far more ornate and elaborate versions of the outfit worn by the peasants.

MAYA MALE WARDROBE

The male Maya peasant wound a cotton loincloth between his legs and several times around his waist. The cloth, called *ex* in the Yucatec tongue, was woven on the home handloom and was around five fingers in width. More elaborate versions of the *ex* were decorated with feathers at each end and, when worn, these hung down colourfully before and behind. Elite men wore loincloths embellished with geometric designs and the heads of deities. Nobles often wore a belt from which they hung jade deity masks and plaques. They might also have worn a god mask on the chest together with a jade-bead necklace.

When he needed protection from the elements, a man wore a square cotton robe over the loincloth. It was held up by knots on the shoulders. This piece of clothing, called a *pati* in Yucatec, was worn plain by the poorest, but was decorated with elaborate embroidery when worn by wealthier members of the community. Rulers often wore a jaguar skin or a *pati* sewn with quetzal feathers to signify their exalted status.

Maya peasants wore deer-hide sandals (*xanch*) tied between the toes and around the ankles with cords of hemp. Nobles wore extremely elaborate sandals with long ties and large heel covers decorated with images of ancestors and deities.

Above: The magnificence of a Maya lord's headdress and chest plate is recreated in this terracotta figure, made c.AD100–650.

Left: Twin statuettes made in Oaxaca AD1150–1250 represent Mixtecs wearing elaborate ear and face jewellery.

MAYA FEMALE WARDROBE

Women in Maya communities wore a loose cotton garment called a *huipil*. In some communities, the *huipil* was a waist-length blouse, worn with a skirt; in others it was a loose, untailored shift-like dress with head and armholes. The *huipil* blouse is worn to this day by Maya women in the mountains of Guatemala: each community has its own distinctive embroidered geometric design. The loose-fitting *huipil* dress is still worn by Maya women in Yucatán, where traditional embroidered designs decorate the hem and the area around the arms and neck. The 16th-century authority Herrera, who reported on the Maya for the Spanish crown, wrote that in his era women wore a loose sack-like dress like the Yucatán *huipil*, together with a cotton headdress. Bishop Diego de Landa wrote that Maya

Above: Musicians and court attendants at Bonampak wear relatively simple costumes but extravagant masks and headdresses.

women wore a simple skirt and a cotton cloth wound around the torso to cover their breasts. Women sometimes also wore a petticoat beneath the *huipil* or skirt, and a shawl over it.

HAIRSTYLES AND BODY ART

Men shaved a small area at the crown of the head, but otherwise kept their hair long, winding it in a plait around the head with the 'tail' dangling down the neck. Luxuriant tresses of black hair were the pride of Maya women, and mothers instructed their growing daughters in caring for their hair and in the many different hairstyles worn. Men and women experimented with body paint and tattoos: the designs worn by women were more delicate than those sported by their husbands and brothers. The colour of body paint could be significant: black indicated that a man was a bachelor, black and red meant a warrior, while black and white was reserved for prisoners. A prayer would be offered for men painted turquoise blue, for they were bound for a fate of ritual slaughter under the priest's sacrificial knife.

Low-ranking men and women wore simple loop earrings made from stone, shell, bone or wood. They embellished their appearance with lip and nose plugs. Elite figures, on the other hand, wore lip plugs, earrings and nose plugs made from obsidian, jade or stone. They also wore a variety of necklaces, collars, bracelets and knee or ankle bands made of jade, feathers, sea or river shells, crocodile teeth and the teeth or claws of the majestic jaguar. After the arrival of metalworking among the Maya in around the 9th century AD, the elite began to wear ornaments and decorations of copper or gold.

ONE ROBE FITS ALL

Among the Aztecs, clothing was also similar among all classes, with the higher social ranks wearing more elaborate garments. Peasant farmers and fishermen often went barefoot and wore a simple loincloth or *máxtlatl*, adding a cloak or *tilmatl* that was knotted over the

Right: Just 14cm (6in) tall, this figurine shows the headdress in great detail.

shoulder when necessary. Among the poor these items were woven from maguey agave fibres, but the wealthier wore cotton. The *tilmatl* might be decorated with animal designs or geometric patterns or have a coloured border. Leading nobles' robes were sometimes feather-covered, bordered with rabbit-fur, dyed turquoise or decorated with jade beads, seashells and pieces of gold. Those in highest authority were permitted to wear a richly coloured waistcoat or *xicolli*.

Nobles wore sandals (*cacli*) usually made of animal skin or woven plant fibres. As among the Maya, these had pronounced heel covers to protect the back of the foot. They also had rubber boots.

Aztec women wore a skirt called a *cúeitl*, wound about the lower body and tied at the waist with a fabric belt. There were regional variations in upper garments. In Tenochtitlán, women wore a waist-length shirt called a *huipil*: the word that is used for the similar Maya garment by scholars is in fact from the Aztecs' Nahuatl tongue. Elsewhere, women tended to wear a cape called a *quechquémitl*.

BEATING THE ODDS

According to Spanish chroniclers, the Aztecs were devoted gamblers. All Mesoamerican games had religious overtones because they saw the entire universe as structured by and charged with divine meaning. Even the apparently chance events of a sporting contest or a gambling pastime were open to interpretation and might provide guidance from the gods.

THE BALL GAME

By far the greatest devotion was reserved for the ball game. It was played in various forms from at least the mid-second millennium BC in Mesoamerica. Two teams of players on an I-shaped earth or stone court tried to send a hard rubber ball through a stone loop set high on one or both walls – or in some versions into the 'end zone' behind their opponents – using elbows, hips and legs. The game was rich in religious symbolism. The ball might be identified with the sun, or the match interpreted as a re-enactment

Left: On the feast of Xocotluetzi, young men competed in climbing the pole to be first to take hold of symbols hanging there.

Above: The test of daring called voladores. *Later, the men will swing upside down around the pole on the end of the ropes.*

of sacred battles between the Aztec gods Quetzalcóatl and Tezcatlipoca or between the Maya Hero Twins and the lords of the underworld. Spectators gambled on the outcome of matches. The game must have been an exhilarating spectacle, played at high speed by very skilled and brave performers wearing elaborate protective costumes. Nevertheless, the ball game was so deeply coloured by its many religious overtones that it was more a religious ceremony than a public sporting contest.

THE BEAN GAME

Another ancient Mesoamerican game of chance and skill, called *patolli* by the Aztecs, was played on the ground using a cross-shaped board of 52 squares painted on a mat or scratched into plaster or clay. Players moved blue and red pieces around the board according to the throw of dice, with the aim of moving all one's pieces to the centre of the cross. The game that developed into *patolli* was played at least as early as the 7th century AD, when a

board was marked out on the floor of the Zacuala residential building in Teotihuacán. About 100–200 years later, no fewer than three boards were marked on the plaster floor of the Palacio Quemado at Tollán.

The cross-shaped Aztec board appears to have been a simplification of an older design incorporating a cruciform shape and squares. *Patolli*, like the ball game, was played throughout Mesoamerica. The Maya marked out playing boards at many ancient sites including Tikal, Uaxactún, Piedras Negras, Chichén Itzá, Palenque and Dzibilchaltún.

In their version of the game, the Aztecs used inscribed kidney beans as their dice – their name *patolli* derives from the Nahuatl word for kidney bean. Both players and onlookers placed wagers: according to a report by Diego Durán, a noisy group would gather around the game and bet on the players. Wealthy merchants and members of the nobility risked large amounts of gold and precious jewels on the outcome; others bet what they could afford. Desperate gamers are said to have bet their house or even their freedom on the result. Durán's report indicated that the game was called *totoloque* and that both playing pieces and dice were made of gold, but scholars believe he must have been mistaken on this last point.

Winning or losing was in the hands of the gods. Durán wrote that players would pray to Macuilxóchitl, god of pleasure and of games, and cast incense into a nearby brazier before making a throw. Sometimes priestly diviners would be asked to interpret the outcome of a throw or of a game. The mat was portable, so the game could be played anywhere, even in the streets. Spanish chroniclers' accounts suggest that *patolli* was played with remarkable and noisy fervour at all hours of night and day in Tenochtitlán.

The Aztecs also played a game resembling checkers on a mat or board marked with squares, using black and white pieces.

POLE GAMES

Two remarkable tests of skill and strength centred on descending or climbing a tall pole. One was a contest associated with the festival of the god Huehuetéotl. Several men competed to be first to reach the top of a very tall pole and grasp an icon of Huehuetéotl that had been placed there.

Another game, dubbed *voladores* ('flyers') by the Spanish conquistadors, involved five men. The five players clambered to the top of a pole. Four attached themselves by one ankle to ropes that were wound elaborately around the pole while the fifth settled himself with flute and drum on a wooden platform at the top of the pole.

As the drummer-flautist played his musical instruments, each of the four flyers leapt headfirst from the pole. Falling upside down, the men would swing round and round by the ankle very fast and getting closer and closer to the ground as the rope unravelled. Just before the flyer smashed his head on the ground, the man would pull himself up on the rope with his hands. This meant that he landed feet-first on the ground – and the momentum then carried him forward at a fast pace. An image from the *Codex Borbonicus* depicts the men circling the pole on ropes to the beat of the drum,

while a priest standing on the steps of a nearby temple pyramid calls down a blessing on the proceedings.

This test of skill as performed by the Aztecs is still attempted in the early 21st century in the Gulf Coast region of Mexico.

Above: Diego Durán gave a full account of patolli *in the* Codex Durán. *This image, from that codex, is of a variant of the game.*

Below: These columns are all that remains of Tollán's Palacio Quemado, where three patolli *boards were marked on the floor.*

MUSIC AND THE BEAT OF THE DRUM

For the Aztecs, music, dancing and singing were among the highest arts. Musicians aspired to be like the great Toltecs of Tollán, masters of every craft and creative art who were celebrated for composing from the very deep places of their hearts and so making music divine. The Aztecs valued dance and music both in profane and sacred contexts, not only as a form of recreation and communal celebration such as in naming ceremonies for children or at marriage feasts, but also as an act of religious devotion, an integral part of ceremonies honouring the gods.

Below: Dressed for ceremonial performance. This carved whistle is from Nebaj, Guatemala, c.AD300–900.

THE SONG HOUSE

Both these forms of music and dance were taught to the young. In the *calmecac* schools of the nobility – where the teachers were priests and where pupils were fledgling rulers, scribes and men of religion – sacred music and ritual dances were taught. In the *telpochcalli* schools frequented by commoners, the future workers of the empire were instructed in love songs, war songs and profane dances. Each of the *telpochcalli* was equipped with a special area called a *cuicalli* ('song house'), consisting of a courtyard surrounded by rooms. The school's highly respected music teacher would place his drums in the centre of the yard and the children would be put through their paces as he played and instructed them in the steps of the dance.

The Spanish churchman Gerónimo de Mendieta, writing in the 16th century, reported that Aztec nobles kept a composer as part of their domestic staff. The composer would write new songs and dances for religious festivals, but also to mark secular events such as a war triumph, a noble wedding or the accession of a new ruler.

DRUMS AND PIPES

Aztec music was stronger on rhythm than on melody: musicians created a strong beat on drums, rattles and rasps. There were two main types of drum: the *huehuetl*, which stood upright, consisted of animal skin stretched over the ends of a carved wooden frame and was played with the hands, while the *teponaxtli*, which was laid horizontally on a circular base, was split to form a double tongue that the drummer hit with rubber-headed hammers to produce a two-tone note. Other musicians complemented the drummers' rhythm with rattles and scrapers made from notched human or animal bone. Wind instruments included conches (large seashells) and flutes, whistles and trumpets (usually made of

Above: This impressivve example of the Aztec huehuetl *('vertical drum') or war drum is carved with warrior imagery.*

clay). Dancers contributed to the music with hand-held gourds filled with seeds, or with anklets of seashells.

The Maya also led their music with rhythm. They had a wide variety of drums. The *tunkul* was, like the Aztec *huehuetl*, an upright drum: the Maya version was made from a hollowed tree trunk and was often as tall as the drummer's chest, with a deerskin stretched over the end. A second Maya drum was identical to the Aztec *teponaxtli*, with two wooden tongues played with hammers, while

Right: Sacred steps in the round. Aztec dancers encircle a minimalist orchestra in this image from the Codex Durán.

another was made from a tortoise shell and played with the palm. Bishop Diego de Landa reported that this tortoise drum gave issue to a very doleful sound. A fourth drum was made from clay and shaped like two vases set base to base, with a membrane at each end. Musicians also played panpipes, conch shells and trumpets of clay or wood. They also had flutes carved from hollowed human leg bones, deer bones and reeds or fashioned from clay. Dancers tied copper, gold or silver bells to their wrists, legs and waist and played a small hand-held drum, called a *pax*, as they danced.

STREET ENTERTAINERS

Music and singing accompanied street entertainments provided by jugglers, acrobats and clowns. Troupes of entertainers laid on dances and comic entertainments for the elite at the courts of rulers and on the spacious patios of noblemen's houses, but also for the commoners in marketplaces, on streets and even outside the cities in small villages. Since trade was performed by barter and currency was little used even at market, they doubtless performed for their supper or for a supply of tortillas, beans and vegetables to take away for later consumption. Hernán Cortés took a troupe of acrobats with him back to Europe, where they performed at the imperial court of Charles V in Spain.

Right: A Mixtec figurine celebrates Macuilxóchitl, patron of the ball game and of the board game patolli, *and god of music.*

FESTIVAL OF THE MUSIC GOD

Macuilxóchitl, who was associated with gambling in his guise as god of pleasure and of games, was also considered to be the patron deity of musicians. He was connected to flower god Xochipilli and to the calendrical day-name '5-flower'.

Macuilxóchitl was sometimes shown with a symbol like a butterfly in place of his mouth. In his role as music god, he might take the form of a turtle. Before his feast day in Tenochtitlán, devotees fasted then covered themselves with jewellery and symbols of the god. According to Bernardino de Sahagún, the ceremony included songs and dancing to the resonant beat of a drum, before worshippers made offerings of animal blood and specially baked cakes to Macuilxóchitl. At the climax of the feast-day celebration, Sahagún reported, priests put a company of slaves to death to satisfy the music god's thirst.

LYRICS AT THE FEAST

Aztec poets found an enthusiastic audience for their work at elite banquets in the leading cities of the empire. Rulers, princes and nobles shared a love of metaphorical language and lyrical self-expression. Masters of verse and philosophical reflection recited their poems in the patio areas of palaces and noble homes, to the accompaniment of music on flutes and drums, while stars danced overhead in the deep blue of night. Most members of the elite classes, including rulers such as Netzahualcóyotl of Texcoco and Tecayehuatzin of Huexotzingo, were poets.

GENRE POETRY

The verses came in a range of genres. One group, known as *xochicuicatl* ('flower songs'), focused on the pleasures and consolations of nature's beauty for those afflicted by suffering. Another group was

THE POET NEZAHUALCÓYOTL
Nezahualcóyotl, ruler of Texcoco, was celebrated as a warrior, wise king and writer of laws. While his forebears and contemporaries were devoted to many gods, he built a temple to a single deity he called Ipalnemoani ('The One By Which We Live') or Tloquenahuaque ('The One Who is Always Near'). He was also a celebrated and sensitive poet, who often examined the pain humans feel due to the changes brought about by the movement of time – which was called *cahuitl* ('the power that departs from us') in the Nahuatl language.

One of his poems declared: 'What can put down lasting roots in this place of change? Everything here is only passing. Even the most precious creations, of jade and turquoise, end in pieces, crumbling to dust.'

yaocuicatl ('war songs'), which expressed a fierce joy in conflict and traced the movements of the mind and heart in battle. *Xopancuicatl* ('spring songs') celebrated the new life of the fields in spring, reminding listeners of the spirit's quickening when maize shoots return after winter. A fourth type were *icnocuicatl* ('orphan songs'). They described the pleasures of life, while recalling the ephemeral nature of all pleasures. One declared: 'The time will come for us all to go, by day or by night, down into the mysteries of death. Here on earth we have time to know ourselves, briefly we pass over the earth's surface.'

The language of the Aztec poets was rich in metaphor. Their poetry was 'song and flowers' bloom'; when a poet

Left: Xochipilli, god of poetry, flowers and souls, was also a symbol of summer. This image is from the Codex Vaticanus.

Above: An unusual portrait of a standing coyote, this stone carving was made by a Totonac sculptor and found at Ihuatzio.

stepped forward to speak he entered into the 'flowering space', the 'spring arena' or the 'house of blooms'. He called political and temporal power 'the place on the mat'.

Tenochtitlán was 'eagle and cactus place' because the México/Aztecs had traditionally founded the city at the spot where they saw an eagle on a cactus, in fulfilment of their god Huitzilopochtli's promise. The city was also 'home of white willows' in reference to the trees that grew there and 'place of darts' because of weapon production in the city.

Poets celebrated warfare as 'shield and dart', 'a singing of shields', and as 'the place where the shields' mist clears'. Poets often spoke of self-knowledge in terms of 'knowing his face'. In Mesoamerican philosophy, the face was seen as the place in which the self resided. Aztec poets could find employment within the religious establishment, as composers of the many hymns – in honour of gods such as Huitzilopochtli, Centéotl, and Tláloc – sung as part of the great religious ceremonies. They also wrote epic poetry, for example the narratives of the birth of the god Huitzilopochtli, of the creation of the world and succession of five world eras, of the many gifts to humankind and the heroic actions of the god-prince Quetzalcóatl.

PUBLIC DEBATE

Another body of literary figures, who may also have been poets, were the *tlamatinime* ('the Ones who Know'). They produced prose works called *huehuehtlahtolli* ('statements of ancient knowledge') that contained philosophical questions, along with statements about duty, death and honour. Sometimes these works were read and debated in public ceremonies. One takes the form of an address by a father to his daughter, in which he warns his offspring that the world is a place of suffering, exhaustion and disappointment, of pain caused by burning sun and winds sharp as obsidian blades. However, he adds that the bitter taste of life is sweetened by compensations such as sensory pleasure, laughter, physical strength and bravery.

A VOICE AT COURT

We have little evidence of the role of Maya scribes in producing poetry and secular writing other than official documents such as the tribute lists, marriage papers or the genealogical histories. However, we know from reports by Diego de Landa and other post-Conquest sources that the Maya enjoyed communal celebrations involving both sacred hymns and secular music with dancing.

The revered *ah ts'ib* or *ah k'u'hun* of Classic Period Maya cities, who proudly wore his pens in his long hair as a status symbol and badge of office, was celebrated for his facility both with language and with images. This exalted figure sat with rulers and their intimates at great state occasions and must surely have given right expression to the feelings of the group in songs and poems. A people that so appreciated the visual arts and music are likely to have been an appreciative audience for the skilful use of words.

Below: This chocolate goblet is decorated with an image of a Maya prince enjoying the drink.

CHAPTER SIX

SACRED CULTURE

Teotihuacán's Temple of Quetzalcóatl, adorned with vast heads of a feathered serpent, was set in a compound containing a plaza large enough to hold a significant proportion of the city's 100,000-plus population. At Chichén Itzá, the Pyramid of Kukulcán also gave on to a vast plaza and was aligned in such a way that thousands of spectators could watch the sun create an astonishing serpentine pattern of light and shadow at spring and autumn equinox. Throughout Mesoamerica, sacred centres were laid out with spectators in mind. At the top of steep steps, positioned scores of metres above the crowd, priests and rulers in bright costumes celebrated the gods in choreographed acts of sacred theatre.

Often this theatre presented acts of sudden or extreme violence – such as slicing open a victim's chest and wrenching out his palpitating heart. However, the sacred drama of religious life also included gentler elements such as dances in celebration of ancestors during the festival of Tlaxochimaco or making corn effigies of the god Xiuhtecuhtli and eating tamales with greens during the festival of Izcalli. Equally, many acts of religious celebration centred on astronomical and seasonal events and effects (as in the equinoctial light show at Chichén Itzá) or on marking the passage of time. Festivities accompanied the end of each *katun* of 7,200 days in Maya cities of the Classic Period such as Tikal and Uaxactún.

Left: The great palace at Palenque commanded views of the city's sacred buildings and ceremonial areas.

THE GAME OF THE GODS

The ball game called *tlachtli* by the Aztecs and *pok-a-tok* by the Maya goes far back into the Mesoamerican past. By the time of the Aztecs it was already at least 2,000 years old, for it was played in Mexico in the mid-second millennium BC. An earthen ball court, 80m (260ft) long and 8m (26ft) wide, at Paso de la Amada in the coastal region of Soconusco, Chiapas, was in use *c.*1400BC and is the oldest court yet discovered in Mesoamerica.

Scholars believe that the game, which was played with a rubber ball, may have originated in the coastal lowlands adjoining the Gulf of Mexico. This was the land of

Below: The ball game's connection to blood-letting fertility rites is plain in this carving from Veracruz depicting a player decapitated after losing a match, with snakes of lifeblood coming from his neck.

rubber and the area in which the Olmec civilization developed in the second to first millennium BC, named in later years from the Nahuatl word *olli* ('rubber'). The design of courts changed over time. The ball court was usually shaped like an 'I', with a thinner central section between two wider end zones. Raised walls usually ran down the sides of the central section and, in many courts, a stone hoop was set in each side wall.

RULES OF THE GAME

Two teams of between two and eleven men each played with a hard, solid rubber ball about 15–20cm (6–8in) in diameter – slightly smaller than a human head.

Players tried to keep the ball moving using only the head, hips, elbows and knees. A team scored points – or in some variants won the match – when one of its players sent the ball through the hoop on the side wall. Stone markers were set at various points of the court, and in some versions players could also score points by hitting these markers or by sending the ball into their opponents' end zone.

The rules must have varied a good deal in different eras and various types of court. In the murals of the Tepantitla residential building in Teotihuacán, artists depicted both the traditional ball game and players competing with hand bats, so the city's residents must have known a bat-and-ball variant of the sport.

Archaeologists also report that at Teotihuacán teams played the traditional ball game on open ground with a few markers to indicate the limits of the pitch and the end zones. The courts had no sidewalls or stone rings and so players

Left: This ceramic figure, found at a site in Nayarit, Mexico, takes part in a variant of the ball game played using hand-held bats.

cannot have scored points by putting the ball through the hoop. Few pitches dating from before AD1100 have been found with side rings on the walls. This element of the game appears to have been an addition of the Postclassic Period.

The ball game was always a great spectacle. The oldest known court, at Pasa de la Amada, was laid out between banks of benches for spectators.

In the Aztec era it was customary for the winners of the game to seize the belongings of the watching crowd – rich pickings, given that the elite turned out bedecked in jewellery and fine robes. There must have been quite a scramble to escape from the seats when the ball passed through the hoop on the side wall and the winning players suddenly poured into the crowd.

A SACRED NARRATIVE

From ancient times the ball game had major religious and ritual significance. Scholars report that the game represented a sacred narrative of the sun god's descent into the underworld, victory there and subsequent ascent as the maize god. Some suggest that a match was played as part of the fertility rites after crop planting, to bring on the rains that fed the maize plants. Carved panels on ball courts often represented maize or cacao plants.

Above: El Tajín had no fewer than 12 ball courts. One court had walls carved with a defeated ballplayer awaiting death, the sacrificial knife poised above his head.

In Aztec lands, the game was associated with the divine history of Quetzalcóatl, the Plumed Serpent god, his descent into the underworld of Mictlán, his out-witting of Mictlantecuhtli and his ascent as the planet Venus. In one version of the myth of Quetzalcóatl-Topiltzin in Tollán, the god played an epic ball game against the god of darkness and fate, Tezcatlipoca, only to lose when the dark lord transformed him into an ocelot.

In Maya regions, the game was an enactment of the exploits of the Hero Twins Hunahpú and Xbalanqué, who played the ball game in the underworld Xibalba against the lords of that place before rising to the heavens as the sun and the planet Venus. It celebrated the divine twins' defeat of the powers of death. Some writers suggest that the ball represented the sun and that the players' attempts to keep it off the ground were part of religious rites designed to honour the sun and maintain its life-giving position in the sky. The ball game represented the ongoing struggle between the powers of light and those of darkness.

SACRIFICIAL GAMES

The ball game was also associated with blood sacrifice. Among both Maya and Aztecs, defeated players could be put to death at the end of the match. Some Maya court complexes included stair-cases: the defeated captain was tied in the shape of a ball and hurled down the steps to death, in celebration of the gods' descent to the underworld. Some author-ities suggest that battles may have been re-enacted through the ball game and that kings or nobles among the prisoners of war were sacrificed at the close of the proceedings.

Rulers either played the game or donned the protective clothing worn by the players for ritual performance. A panel at La Amelia in Guatemala shows the King of Dos Pilas wearing a ball game outfit of kneepads and belt, while a ball court carving at Copán represents the king as a ball-playing Hero Twin. Like the board game *patolli*, the ball game could be an act of divination. In some accounts, Moctezuma II was defeated in a match against Netzahualpilli, the ruler of Texcoco, who had prophesied that a foreign race would govern Tenochtitlán. Moctezuma's defeat was one of many ill omens that unsettled the ruler before the arrival of Hernán Cortés.

Below: Players face up for a round of the ball game in an image from the Codex Borbonicus. *The Nahuatl word* tlachtli *also meant the I-shaped court on which it was played.*

CYCLES OF TIME

Mesoamericans believed the universe was constructed according to a sacred pattern that could be read in the movements of the stars, and of time through its units of hours and days. Priests and astronomers kept astonishingly accurate track of time using the movement of the stars as their measure. The long, recurring patterns of the night sky provided a physical template of the invisible patterns of time.

OBSERVING TIME IN THE SKIES

These highly skilled astronomers apparently used the simplest of observational equipment, judging the movements of the stars with the naked eye against

Below: One of the windows in the Caracol tower at Chichén Itzá is aligned to the setting of the sun on the vernal equinox.

notches cut in a pair of crossed sticks. Sacred structures and complexes of buildings were laid out to honour celestial and calendrical events such as solstices and equinoxes and to aid in their observation. For example, the Pyramid of the Sun at Teotihuacán was aligned to mark the sun's daily east–west passage and the equinoctial rising of the Pleiades constellation on the horizon.

At Uaxactún the pyramids and temples labelled Group E by scholars were precisely arranged to enable astronomical observation to be made and celebrated. On the western side of a plaza stood a single pyramid, while opposite, on top of a platform on the eastern side, were three temples – E-I (at the platform's northern edge), E-II (in the platform's centre and so due east of the pyramid) and E-III (at

Above: A detail of a stone carving from Chichén Itzá represents Noh Ek (Great Star), the symbol of the planet Venus.

the platform's southern edge). An astronomer standing on top of the pyramid on the western side of the plaza would have viewed the sun rise directly above temple E-I on the June 21 solstice, directly above temple E-III on the December 21 solstice and precisely over temple E-II on the midpoints of 21 March and 23 September. This remarkably precise layout was the prototype for other building complexes in Maya cities of the Classic Period.

INTERSECTING CYCLES

Astronomers plotted the 584-day cycle of the planet Venus and its interaction with the 365-day solar pattern and calculated that the two intersected every 2,920 days – equivalent to eight solar years or five Venus cycles. Occasions on which holy cycles interconnected in this way were doubly sacred and were the occasion for grand ceremonies. Another example is the intersection once every 52 solar years of the *tonalpohualli* day count and the *xiuhpohualli* year count. The end of a 52-year cycle – called a 'bundle of years' by the Aztecs – was a time of potential calamity, with the prospect of universal dissolution should the gods choose not to inaugurate a new bundle of years. The new cycle in turn was a time of renewal and optimism, in which pyramids and ceremonial buildings might be refaced with stone and householders rebuilt or refurbished their homes.

THE MAYA LONG COUNT

The Maya also marked time using a longer-running measure that scholars label the Maya Long Count. Dates were marked on stelae, stone thrones and other monuments in Maya cities of the Classic Period to commemorate royal births and accessions to the throne, battle victories, ritual sacrifices of rival leaders and so on.

Time was counted forward from a date zero that corresponds to 11 August 3114BC in the Gregorian calendar and dates were carved in five units of decreasing size: 144,000 days (*baktun*), 7,200 days (*katun*), 360 days (*tun*), 20 days (*uinal*), and 1 day (*kin*). Kings set up monuments to mark the end of each *katun*, which was a time of public festivity. The elite and people of Uaxactún held a *katun*-end festival in AD357 – or 8.16.0.0.0. in the Long Count. Rulers also erected monuments to mark the halfway point in a

Below: This pyramid is one of the temple-observatories of Group E at Uaxactún, aligned to view sunrise on the solstices.

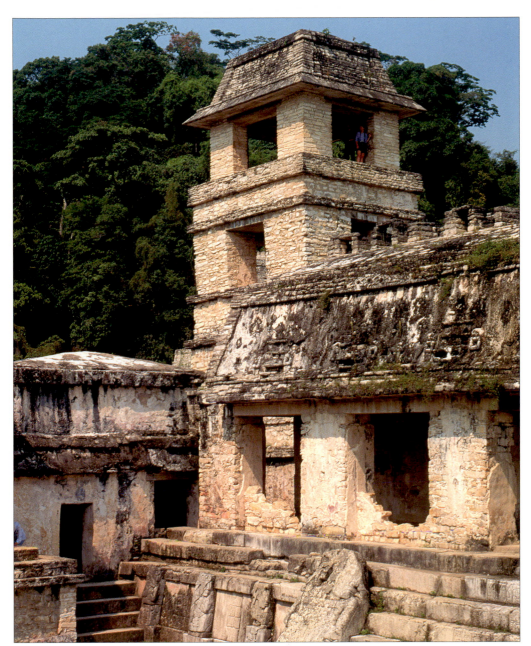

Above: The four-storey tower in the Palace complex at Palenque was probably used as an observatory by the king's astronomers.

katun – a period of 3,600 days known as a *lahuntun*. At Piedras Negras and Quiriguá, rulers even marked the passing of the quarter-*katun* timespan of 1,800 days (*hotun*).

Katuns came in cycles of 13, totalling 93,600 days or around 256 years. Each *katun* of the 13 was identified by number and associated with a set of prophecies: diviners, rulers and ordinary people expected a *katun* to contain events and conditions similar to those in a past *katun* of the same number.

This temporal repetition could be bad or good, unwelcome or welcome. Kings at Tikal in particular went to great lengths to emphasize their connection through the cycle of *katuns* to an earlier period of material wealth.

THE HOLY COUNT

Certain numbers had profound religious symbolism. Three was a holy number because the universe had three layers: the heavens, the terrestrial plane and the underworld. Thirteen, the number of planes in the heavens, was also sacred, as was nine, the number of layers in the dark underworld. Divine figures had power over each of these layers. According to Yucatec-speaking Maya, the gods of heaven were *oxlahuntiku* (combining the words for 'god', *ku*, with that for 'thirteen', *oxlahun*) and the lords of the underworld were *bolontiku* (from 'nine', *bolon*).

HOLY WORLD, SACRED SKY

Ancient religious life in Mesoamerica was focused on the fertility of the earth and led by shamans who assumed animal form to undertake spirit voyages. In the religious tradition that grew from these roots, the earth and heavens were sacred, patterned with divine meaning.

NATURAL AND SUPERNATURAL
Mesoamericans saw no clear distinction between the material world in one place and the spirit world in another. The physical world of deserts, rivers, seas, mountains, storms, maize plants, great trees, wild animals and people was built according to the sacred template that also structured the movements of celestial planets and the cycles of time. Diviners could interpret earthly events and celestial movements in terms of time's patterns and future events. The movements of celestial bodies such as the sun and Venus gave sacred meaning to the physical forms of the earth. For example, some Maya traditions understood the four directions in terms of the movements of the sun. The east was the place of

Below: Mesoamericans saw sacred wells, such as this one at Chichén Itzá, as an opening into the underworld of the spirits.

Above: This stone turtle was carved by an Olmec craftsman before 200BC. The Maya believed the earth rested on a turtle's back.

the sun's morning emergence from the underworld and the west the place of its evening descent to the dark Xibalba, place of death. The north was the sun's full power at the zenith, its position at noon, while the south was identified with

SACRED PLANTS
In Aztec lands tobacco was called *yetl*, and was said to have been created in the celestial realms for the gods' enlightenment. Priests smoked the plant in animal-headed clay pipes in an attempt to call on the god whose animal form was depicted by the pipe bowl. For example, a pipe with a dog's head might be used to summon Xólotl, the twin form of Quetzalcóatl, who took the shape of a dog.

In Maya ceremonies in Yucatán, priests rolled great cigars of tobacco and drank a wine made from the bark of the balche tree. Experts report that they used wild tobacco with a nicotine content of 16 per cent, a full 16 times stronger than that smoked in typical Western cigarettes.

Mesoamericans also held holy a number of hallucinogenic mushrooms (for example, *psilocybe aztecorum*) as well as the maguey cactus, whose fermented sap was made into the alcoholic drink *pulque*.

Above: A wall painting at Chichén Itzá, c. AD900, *depicts the ancient plumed serpent god known to the Maya as Kukulkán.*

the darkest hour of midnight, when the sun fights for its very life with the lords of the underworld.

In the night sky, the Maya saw the Milky Way as a vast two-headed sky serpent, with one head giving issue to life and the other the source of death. The serpent appears to have been an embodiment of the supreme Maya god Itzamná or Hunab Ku. In this form, Itzamná gave issue from one mouth in the east to the rising sun, bringer of life, while from his second mouth in the west death came with the swallowing of the sun. The Milky Way was also a pathway to the underworld. In Yucatec it was called *Zac Beh* ('The White Path') and was understood to be the road followed by the spirits of the deceased as they travelled to the underworld to face a series of demanding tests.

Mesoamericans saw mountains as sacred; a physical form for the celestial home of ancestors according to Maya traditions, a source of life according to Aztec beliefs. The Aztecs identified mountains as the places of the rain god Tláloc's stores of water, the origin of the maize plant discovered in the mountain's heart by Quetzalcóatl and the place of the tribal lord Huitzilopochtli's birth. A cave in a rocky, dusty mountainside was

a place of burial, an entrance to the sacred earth and a place of access to the land of the revered ancestors.

Aztec and Maya cities replicated these sacred physical forms in stone. The temple was a holy mountain and its entrance was a sacred cave. The ball court, also like a holy cavern, represented an entrance to the underworld.

ANIMAL ALLIES

The sacred patterning extended to the world of animals. Many creatures were held to be holy because they were forms of the gods. Tezcatlipoca might be the majestic jaguar or the cunning coyote; Huitzilopochtli was eagle, hummingbird or macaw, Quetzalcóatl – or Kukulcán in Maya lands – was quetzal as well as divine serpent. The turtle, the crocodile and the snake were images of the fertile earth.

Mesoamericans also believed that humans had animal protectors or familiars known as *nahual* in the Aztec language and as *way* by many Maya groups. These were

Right: This figure made by a Remojadas potter in Veracruz, c.600–900AD, *wears a jaguar-head belt and may represent a shaman.*

the creatures whose forms shamans might adopt. They would do this upon entering a state of instructive spiritual ecstasy under the influence of one of the plants held to be sacred for their power to transport seekers beyond the boundaries of everyday consciousness.

THE HEALING ARTS

To the Aztecs healing was sacred: their main word for doctor, *teopati*, combined *patli* ('medical arts') and *teo* ('holy'). Aztec creation narrative explained the cause of sickness. At the start of the fifth or current world age, the existing race of humankind was made from the bones of the men and women who had lived in the fourth world age. These bones had been languishing in the underworld, but the Feathered Serpent god Quetzalcóatl ventured into that dark realm to rescue them. However, the Feathered Serpent was tricked during his escape from the

underworld and dropped the bones, which broke into many pieces. He carried the remains to the home of the gods, where all the divine lords and ladies agreed that the bones should be ground to a powder, then moistened with the gods' blood and mixed to a paste. From this paste the first people of the fifth world age were made. People suffered illness, old age and death because they were originally made from broken bones. However, they had a special calling to serve the gods because they were fashioned from the gods' blood.

THREE SPIRIT CENTRES

People were made according to the same divine template that structured all parts of the universe. Just as the universe had a tripartite structure – with the heavens above, the terrestrial plane in the middle and the underworld beneath – so three spirit centres existed within the human body. The first, residing in the head, was *tonalli* ('hotness'). This was the counterpart of the soaring heavens.

When a body lost *tonalli*, death followed – and so a corpse was cold. People dissipated *tonalli* by self-indulgence in sex or drunkenness. They could boost it by bravery in battle and by living an austere, self-restrained life. Doctors sometimes prescribed herbal fragrances to increase a patient's *tonalli*. In the natural way of things, *tonalli* increased with age and old people were respected for having a strong *tonalli*. When a shaman or diviner embarked on a spirit voyage, it was his *tonalli* that left his body and entered another realm.

The second spirit centre, *teyolia*, was the counterpart of the terrestrial plane and was situated in the heart. *Teyolia* was the source of our thoughts, creative impulses and human personality. Tenochtitlán's noble poets were rich in the quality of *teyolia*. This, too, was weakened by sensual indulgence. The *teyolia* was akin to the Western idea of the soul in that it departed the body at death and travelled to its fate in the afterlife – the underworld for most, but one of the levels of heaven for those who had been sacrificed, killed in battle, died giving birth or suffered various watery deaths associated with the rain god Tláloc.

The third spirit centre, *ihiyotl*, situated in the liver, was the counterpart of the underworld. Energy, life's breath and

Left: The Florentine Codex *(1575–77) depicts various Aztec medical procedures, including a cure for haemorrhoids, treating a fever and the binding of a broken leg.*

passionate desire were the products of *ihiyotl*. Lazy people, who lacked drive and the power to achieve things, were understood to have a badly functioning *ihiyotl*.

A HEALTHY BALANCE

The three parts of the universe were perpetually held in balance by natural order, by the four cardinal directions and by the tree of life that majestically rose in the centre of the universe connecting heaven, earth and underworld. Doctors taught that the way to health lay in safeguarding the good functioning of the three spirit centres of the body and ensuring a natural balance between them. An unexpected reverse or accident might damage one of the centres and cause illness or disturbed behaviour. For example, a shock resulting in emotional turmoil would be expected to damage a person's *ihiyotl*.

SPIRITUAL HEALING

Throughout Mesoamerica healing combined knowledge of herbal remedies with trust in the power of shamans and diviners to seek and remedy the causes of health problems. In addition, all peoples of Mesoamerica put faith in the power of public bloodletting and sacred ritual to

satisfy the gods and avert disease, famine, earthquake and other natural disasters. Physical and spiritual were intertwined: illnesses or disturbances might have physical or spiritual causes and could be treated with spiritual or physical means, or both. A doctor might tell a woman with a severe cold that she had suffered damage to her *tonalli*. He could use his knowledge of herbal medicine to prescribe a fragrance to boost her *tonalli*. Equally, he might seek out the spiritual cause of the malaise by sending her to a diviner.

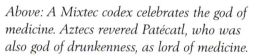

Above: A Mixtec codex celebrates the god of medicine. Aztecs revered Patécatl, who was also god of drunkenness, as lord of medicine.

The diviner would seek to discover whether the damage to the woman's *tonalli* was caused by a curse from one of the gods. Sometimes the diviner might take hallucinogenic mushrooms, peyote or morning glory seeds to bring on a trance in which he could discover the cause and find a way to appease the god in question. He might throw coral seeds and seek answers from the movement of sensations in his body.

Aztec doctors were divided broadly into those treating physical symptoms, the *teopati*, and those seeking and addressing spiritual causes, *tictli*, men who could read the divine patterns and structures of the universe. The medical specialists were expert in herbal medicine, the *tlametpatli*, who drew on their ancient healing art to treat problems including heart trouble, stomach sickness and breathing disorders. In markets across the empire, *panamacanis* sold mixed herbal remedies.

Left: A detail from the Florentine Codex *shows a plant used to treat fever. Healers administered bitter medicines wrapped in chocolate paste to patients.*

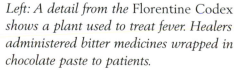

SACRED THEATRE

Large-scale public sacrifices on the steps of temple pyramids made a powerful statement of secular power as well as of religious devotion. In Tenochtitlán, visiting dignitaries witnessed an over-whelming proof of the city's great power, which was sufficient to build the vast sacred arena, mobilize a cadre of magnificently attired priests and musicians and bring to sacrifice a vast army of prisoners.

RITES OF SACRIFICE

The crowds which gathered for the ceremony celebrated the power of the gods who demanded and were worthy of such ritual; the glory of the ruler who could command such a display; and – a central

Above: At Chichén Itzá the Temple of the Feathered Serpent – viewed here from the top of the Temple of the Warriors – was an awe-inspiring setting for sacred ritual.

mystery of their religion – the fact that life was dependent on sacrifice. Just as, in Aztec belief, the gods had sacrificed their blood to the creation of humans in the current age and then again to set the sun moving in the sky, so human blood was a necessary offering to maintain sacred order and balance in the cosmos.

Public rites of sacrifice brought the gods to visible life on the temple steps or in sacred processional. A priest or ruler dressed as the god or goddess honoured became that divine form. A priestess wearing a jade skirt was Chalchiúhtlicue in Tenochtitlán, while a Maya ruler might embody the maize god or Chac, lord of rains. Equally, victims destined for sacrifice were considered by the Aztecs to be *ixiptla* ('in the gods' image'). They were believed to contain within their frail human bodies the awesome power of creation and destruction that belonged to the gods,

Right: A detail from the Codex Mendoza *(c.1541) shows part of a sacred ritual as a priest plays drums and sings hymns.*

making possible the re-enactment of the primal scenes of divine sacrifice through which this world's sun and people were brought into being.

The Toltecs and their followers in Tenochtitlán and Chichén Itzá greatly escalated the use of ritual slaughter in religious ceremonies. From the era of Tollán onwards, human sacrifice had a much greater role.

RITUAL SONGS

The Aztecs sang hymns to honour their gods during religious ceremonies. Sacred songs have survived to the goggle-eyed rain god Tláloc, to flower god Xochipilli, to strong-limbed maize deities Chicomecóatl and Centéotl and to the war lord Huitzilopochtli. The hymn in praise of Xochipilli declares that the sacred quetzal bird sings its joy in the flower lord during the dark hours of midnight, while the worshipper makes his song at dawn, adding that praise will rise to Xochipilli from Tláloc's temple.

Tláloc's hymn praises the god as a magician and envisages ancestors at rest or playing at ball in the misty paradise of Tlálocan. Huitzilopochtli's hymn celebrates him as the sun god, who lives among the clouds and the cold air, who as he spreads the brilliance of light stirs a passion for war in the hearts of men. The song, which was probably declaimed by two singers in a stirring answer and response, hails Huitzilopochtli as the instigator of sacred conflicts that result in the defeat and capture of many prisoners for holy sacrifice.

particular musical ceremonies in which they specialized. De Landa described one dance in which two men led the steps. One hurled reeds at the other, who exhibited great skill in catching them, all the while following the steps of the dance. Another dance witnessed by de Landa was a sacred war dance, in which as many as 800 men carrying small banners followed a complex pattern of steps in perfect unison. In Tenochtitlán, the leading warriors, priests and members of the *pipiltin* nobility engaged in a sacred dance with their divine ruler at the climax of enthronement ceremonies that began the rule of a new *tlatoani*.

Below: In the gods' image. A Maya funerary urn, c.AD250–900, represents a fearsome-looking priest dressed in ritual costume.

Above: Offering plate. A chacmool from Tenochtitlán holds the hollowed dish used to display the hearts of sacrificial victims.

INCENSE AND DANCING

Ceremonies were accompanied by the burning of incense, usually copal resin, but also the resin of the rubber and chicle trees. Worshippers believed that as the smoke rose it became food for the gods and goddesses. In sacrifices to placate the rain god, his human petitioners told that the clouds of incense had the power to attract the dark, rain-heavy clouds for which they prayed. Before burning, cakes of resin were painted turquoise blue, the colour of sacrifice. When worshippers could not provide a jaguar or alligator for animal sacrifice, the incense was sometimes moulded into the shape of an animal heart. In the Cenote of Sacrifice at Chichén Itzá, a worshipper made an offering of an incense ball containing a cake of vegetable material in the shape of a human heart.

Music played an important role in the theatre of the sacred. Large bands of musicians took part in sacred processions and sacrificial ceremonies, playing clay and shell trumpets, drums and rattles, and creating a mournful howl with conch shells. The celebrated murals at Bonampak represented a 12-man orchestra as part of a procession: they played tortoise-shell drums, ceramic trumpets and seed-filled gourds.

Among the Maya, group dances were very serious and highly sacred. According to Bishop Diego de Landa, groups of men and women danced separately and had

THE ROUND OF FESTIVALS

The Aztecs believed that they were dependent on the gods for the sun's rising every morning, and wove rites of religious observance into the very fabric of daily life. Each of the eighteen 20-day months had at least one festival honouring the gods. These were not all of equal importance to an individual. People with skilled occupations, for instance, had their patron gods and observed ceremonies with particular attention at the time

Left: A statue of Xipe Totec from Veracruz c.AD900–1200 shows a priest who is wearing a flayed skin.

when their patron was celebrated. Among the people of the empire, so many of whom worked on the land, the more ancient fertility-based cults of such gods and goddesses as Tláloc, Chalchiúhtlicue and Centéotl would probably have had more impact than the newer cult of Huitzilopochtli, which was associated with the elite.

CYCLE OF AZTEC FESTIVALS

For a farmer in the Tenochtitlán *chinampa* fields, the festivals associated with the stages of the agricultural year loomed largest. In the first month of the Aztec year (14 February–5 March), worshippers at the festivals of Atlcaualo ('The Ending of Water') and Cuauhitleua ('The Lifting of Trees') made offerings to maize goddesses Chicomecóatl and Xilonen. These included sacrifices of children.

In the second month (6 March–25 March), during the festival of Tlacaxipehualiztli ('Skinning of the Men'), sacrificial victims were killed and skinned in honour of Xipe Totec, god of spring and germinating seeds. The god's priests wore the skin of a victim over their own face and body. In the fourth month

Above: Sacred serpents and presiding deities are detailed in one of the 56 almanac pages of the Maya Madrid Codex.

(15 April–4 May), as part of Huey Tozoztli ('Major Vigil'), priestesses of Chicomecóatl performed rites to bring the gods' blessing on farmers' seed supplies.

In the eighth month (4 July–23 July), the festival of Huey Tecuilhuitl ('Major Festival of the Lords') celebrated the appearance in the fields of the first shoots of maize and particularly honoured Xilonen, the goddess associated with these shoots. Offerings were made to a young woman who took the form of Xilonen for the duration of the festival.

Harvest was celebrated in the eleventh and twelfth months (2 September–21 September; 22 September–11 October'), in the festivals of Ochpaniztli ('Clearing) and Teotleco ('Coming of the Gods and Goddesses'). In the first of these, a female victim was killed and flayed in honour of Xilonen-Chicomecóatl and her skin worn by a priestess of the goddesses, in grim echo of the festival of Tlacaxipehualiztli. The second festival was a simpler celebration of the harvest.

No doubt overshadowing all these festivals in the mind of the farmer was the one that marked the end of a 52-year cycle of the 260- and 365-day calendars and the beginning of a new cycle. It usually occurred once only – if at all – in a lifetime. On the night in question, the most senior priests sacrificed a victim on Mount Huixachtlán ('Place of the Thorn Trees'), cut his chest, then tore out his heart and in his gaping chest cavity lit a new fire signifying the new cycle of years. If the new fire did not take, according to religious teaching, it showed that the gods did not consent to allow a new cycle to commence and the current age of the world, in which the Aztec empire had grown to glory, would end.

Below: A deity consumes the flesh of a sacrificial victim in a detail from an Aztec tonalamatl *book of days.*

CYCLE OF MAYA FESTIVALS

The Maya laid out large and important complexes of buildings in major cities of the Classic Period to celebrate equinoxes and solstices. Occasions such as the year's shortest and longest days were charged with sacred meaning and were the focus of ritual public celebration.

Our main source for detailed knowledge of the festivals of the Maya year is the account given by Bishop Diego de Landa of religious ceremonies in 16th-century Yucatán. As with the Aztec calendar, the year ended with five days of ill renown when people tried to avoid activity. The new year and beginning of the first month, Pop, was celebrated by sweeping houses and replacing all household tools and utensils. The second month, Uo, was the time for fishermen, hunters, doctors

Above: A flint sacrificial knife symbolically stops the life breath in a ritual victim's skull. This offering is from Tenochtitlán.

and priests to celebrate their patron gods; the priests performed acts of divination using the sacred books to read the fates for the coming year. In the fifth month, Tzec, beekeepers made offerings to Hobnil, one of the four *bacabs* said to support the creation in the four cardinal points. They burned incense and prayed to be granted large amounts of honey. In the sixth month, Xul, offerings were made to Kukulcán, the Feathered Serpent. A great procession with feather banners culminated in offerings of food at Kukulcán's temple; devotees stayed at the temple for five days, while jesters toured the town putting on performances and collecting contributions that were then divided between the nobility, the priests and the jesters themselves.

During the eleventh month, Zac, hunters made offerings to atone for the blood they had spilled as they went about their work. In the thirteenth month, Mac, a large-scale sacrifice of animals was performed in honour of Itzamná and the four rain gods or Chacs to ensure plentiful rainfall to feed the maize plants in the approaching rainy season. In the sixteenth month, Pax, a war ceremony was held that culminated in feasting, drinking and sacred dances.

THE CULT OF VIOLENCE

Mesoamericans saw conflict as a sacred and ubiquitous element of life. As the sun rose each morning, it slaughtered the moon and stars that had proudly ruled the night sky just as, the Aztecs said, proud Huitzilopochtli had killed the moon goddess Coyolxauhqui and his four hundred brothers in the first moments of life. The shedding of sacrificial blood was a sacred duty; a way of maintaining universal order by honouring the blood sacrifice offered by the gods that had brought the current world age into being.

Sacrifice and warfare were intimately connected; indeed, military conflict was a sacrament. Warfare was celebrated as an opportunity to demonstrate character, bravery and power and as a means of feeding the gods' thirst for blood. A major impetus for warfare was the need for sacrificial victims.

Below: A detail from the late 16th-century Codex Magliabechano shows a bloody sacrifice in honour of Tezcatlipoca during the Aztecs' 13th month, Pachtontli.

Among the Maya, commoner prisoners may have been made into slaves, but nobles, leading warriors and – most significantly – rival rulers were destined for ritual public sacrifice. The Maya considered human sacrifice to be a necessary rite for major events such as the inauguration of a new king's reign, the first use of a new temple or building and the announcement, birth or blessing of an heir to the throne.

KILLING KINGS

In Classic Period Maya cities, a special decapitation ceremony was reserved for the despatch of captured kings and rulers. Such a sacrifice was recorded in carving by a glyph called the 'axe event' by scholars. A ball court marker erected by King Kan II of Caracol commemorates the sacrifice by 'axe event' of a Caracol ruler in AD556 in the rival city of Tikal, a sacrifice that sparked a conflict between Caracol and Tikal. The

Below: Sacrificial ritual mirrored the ferocity of the wild. This jaguar statue is from Chichén Itzá.

conflict ended in a Caracol victory in AD562 and, probably, in the sacrificial beheading of Tikal ruler Double Bird. The decapitation sacrifice may have occurred as the climax of a ritual enactment of the ball game, which celebrated the triumph of the Hero Twins in defeating the lords of Xibalba.

Among the Maya of the Postclassic Period in cities such as Chichén Itzá, victims were painted turquoise blue, the colour of sacrifice, and led up the temple steps to the sacrificial platform wearing peaked headgear. There, high above the crowds watching in the plaza below, the sacrificial stone was painted turquoise and four assistant priests, also dressed in this brilliant colour, held the victim over the stone while the main priest or *chilan* carved open the victim's chest and wrenched out his heart. The *chilan* then smeared statues of the gods being honoured with the heart blood of the sacrificial victim and wiped the blood on his own skin. He cast the body down the steep steps into the plaza, where it was skinned by helpers. The skin was given back to the *chilan*, who put it on as a 'suit' and danced before the crowd.

The Maya of Chichén Itzá had adopted the Mexican sacrificial practice, presumably the one followed by the Toltecs. Aztec priests of this era also tore the heart from the chest of a sacrificial victim. After

Above: A ritual victim's death was highly honourable. The Codex Duran *(1570–81) shows a team of Aztec priests extracting a human heart on the sacrificial stone.*

holding it up in offering to the sun god Tonatiuh, they threw it at the image of the god being celebrated, Huitzilopochtli or Tláloc, which in time became covered with the blood of the victims. In the plaza below, the audience in this theatre of sacred violence watched the rite and saw blood run down the steps of the temple platform while the bodies of the victims were cast down to tumble over the slick steps until they reached bottom.

DEATH BY RITUAL CONFLICT
Both Maya and Aztecs also performed sacrifices through ritualized conflict. In the Aztec festival of Tlacaxipehualiztli ('Skinning of the Men'), held in the second month in honour of Xipe Totec, Aztec warriors bearing clubs fitted with razor-sharp obsidian blades attacked victims tied to a sacrificial stone who were armed only with a club decorated with feathers. The warriors slashed at the defenceless 'combatants' until their blood ran freely into the earth.

A similar stylized conflict was performed as a rite of sacrifice by the Maya. The victim was stripped naked, painted turquoise blue and dressed in the peaked headdress associated with sacrifice. He was tied to a post while warriors danced around him, each bearing a bow and arrows. A priest took blood from the victim's genitals and made offering of it to the gods. Then the warriors began to shoot, sending a hail of arrows at the chest of the victim until he slumped lifeless on the spot.

A graffito drawn in Temple II at Tikal depicts a similar sacrifice of a victim tied to a sacrificial post and slain by a magnificently attired warrior-priest who is using either an arrow or a spear.

REVERENCE FOR ANCESTORS

Long after its decline from power, the city of Chichén Itzá was a major destination for pilgrims from throughout Maya territories. They came to offer sacrifices in the great Cenote of Sacrifice and to wonder at the magnificent temple of Kukulkán, the immense ball court and the vast hall of the thousand columns. Here, as in highland Mexico, the present seemed unable to match the achievements of the past.

The México/Aztecs who founded Tenochtitlán were part of a wave of incomers from the barren north. Insecure as newcomers and as nomads with no evidence of past achievement, they attempted to find glory by association through linking themselves to the Toltecs and Tollán, even claiming that they had spent some years among the holy ruins of that city during their southward migration; the older ruined city of Teotihuacán the Aztecs saw as a place of the gods, site of sacred events at the start of the current world age. They made pilgrimages to both Tollán and Teotihuacán, bringing offerings to place in the sacred spaces of those cities, adding their own religious structures on the hallowed ground and also removing items left by the ancestors and carrying these objects back to sanctify sacred buildings in Tenochtitlán.

Aztec mourners buried two people with pottery from Tenochtitlán and Texcoco in part of the Ciudadela at

Right: This stone mask was part of a noble burial in Teotihuacán c. AD400. Many masks were later reused by the Aztecs.

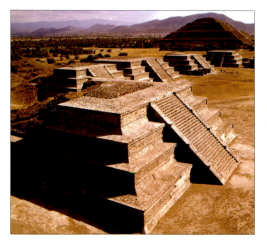

Left: The scale of Teotihuacán's sacred architecture overawed later Mesoamericans. Surrounding the Plaza of the Moon, once a scene of ritual worship, are eleven temples.

Teotihuacán; Aztec architects even built a pyramid-platform over and encompassing the pyramid-temple of Quetzalcóatl there.

At Tollán Aztec religious visitors made similar burials and ceramic offerings, and also built residential quarters and sacred structures on top of the ceremonial centre of the Toltecs. Funerary masks from Teotihuacán graves were laid as offerings within the Templo Mayor in Tenochtitlán.

SACRED GIFTS

Throughout Mesoamerica, people of the Post-Classic Period performed religious rites and made offerings before or within great sacred sculptures of earlier times. In Morelos in the 13th century pilgrims made offerings before the great 2,000-year-old Olmec carvings at Chalcatzingo: local Tlahuica builders erected stairways and platforms to a height of 30m (100ft) to create a sacred space before the carving known as Monument 2, which represents a reclining figure with two people wearing elaborate ceremonial garb approaching him and one moving away. At Monté Albán, Mixtec pilgrims buried their rulers and in the grave known by archaeologists as Tomb 7 left magnificent offerings of gold and silverwork. Maya pilgrims conducted religious ceremonies and left ceramic effigies in the ruined temples at the Classic Period site of Dzibanché, Quintana Roo.

A SACRED TRADITION

In venerating ancient objects, reusing them and making offerings of them in tombs and temples, the peoples of the 12th–15th centuries AD were following a very well-established Mesoamerican religious tradition. Many centuries earlier, at Classic Period cities such as Tikal, Uaxactún and Cozumel, devotees made offerings of Olmec figurines, masks, plaques and objects used for drawing one's own blood. Maya nobles or rulers in this era wore Olmec greenstone pieces as sacred amulets.

A PILGRIMAGE GONE WRONG

In 1536 Ah Dzun Xiu, descendant of the Xiu dynasty that had been ousted by their rivals the Cocoms at Chichén Itzá in the 13th century, determined to lead a pilgrimage to make human sacrifices at the Sacred Cenote in the city of his ancestors. The king, who now ruled in the city of Mani, had been convinced by a recent hurricane, plague and smallpox epidemic that there was a pressing need to appease the gods. He asked for a guarantee of safe passage through the lands of his traditional enemy, Nachi Cocom. The lord of the Cocoms granted the request but plotted violence. When Ah Dzun Xiu, his son, nobles and trains of sacrificial victims arrived in Cocom lands, they were lavishly welcomed with feasting and entertainments that lasted for four whole days. But on the fourth evening, the hosts turned suddenly and viciously on their guests and slaughtered every last one. The gods had their sacrifice, but without the ceremony that had been planned. The episode served further to divide the Maya of Yucatán and paved the way for victory in the region by a force of Spanish conquistadors.

PILGRIMS TO THE PYRAMIDS

Surviving documents from the 16th century indicate that the Aztecs used the Teotihuacán pyramids not just for reverent worship, making offerings and blood sacrifices, but also as a dramatic setting in which to execute criminals. One account reports that on the Teotihuacán pyramids Tenochtitlán priests set up images of the underworld god Mictlantecuhtli, of the moon goddess Coyolxauhqui and of Tonacatecuhtli (Lord of our Sustenance), the male aspect of the primeval god of duality Ometéotl. The priests came in the company of the *tlatoani* once every month in their calendar – that is, every 20 days – to seek the gods' continued blessings on the growing empire. Priests and worshippers also sought guidance at oracle shrines in the ancient city. Aztecs deeply respectful of the achievements of the past also visited the ruins of the fortified city of Xochicalco, in western Morelos, where they reverently viewed the carvings of serpents, hieroglyphs and humans on the Pyramid of the Feathered Serpent.

Aztec potters and stonemasons expressed their devotion to the sacred power of the past and respect for the achievements of their ancient forebears by imitating bygone styles. At Tenochtitlán a group of heads of the *xiucóatl* ('fire-serpent') accompanied by calendrical dates is a homage to Xochicalco's Pyramid of

Above: Many generations of Mesoamericans revered their Olmec forebears. This head of an Olmec king is now at Villahermosa.

the Feathered Serpent. Sculptors also produced statues celebrating sacred images from Teotihuacán, while builders copied the proportions, murals and decorative style of Teotihuacán when constructing the five diminutive buildings in Tenochtitlán called the Red Temples. The nearby House of the Eagles, which lay just to the north of the Templo Mayor, was a detailed celebration of the achievements of Toltec stonemasons, sculptors and woodworkers.

Below: Many sacred structures at Chichén Itzá were built to honour the architecture and religious culture of the Toltecs. This is a detail of the Platform of the Eagles.

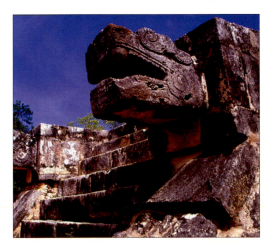

WHERE THE ANCESTORS GO

The Aztecs were taught not to fear death. Life and death were one aspect of the sacred duality that structured the universe, a duality also expressed in oppositions such as day and night, hot and cold, light and darkness.. Life was not easy, suffering was inevitable and death was inescapable. Many deaths were celebrated as honourable, for example, dying in giving birth, in battle or in a rite of human sacrifice. For the Aztecs it was a matter of honour to embrace death with equanimity and with a certain pride.

DAY OF THE DEAD

The Aztecs' positive attitude to death has carried through into modern Mexican celebrations on the Day of the Dead.

The Day of the Dead is celebrated on the Roman Catholic Church feasts of All Saints' Day (1 November) and All Souls' Day (2 November). The first day is usually set aside to remember those who died in childhood and infancy, with departed adults celebrated on the second day.

At home people build small altars in memory of the dead and load them with food, drinks, cakes and sweets – including sweet rolls called *pan de muerto* ('death bread') adorned with dough pieces shaped like bones, and breads called *anima* ('souls'), as well as a cup of the traditional maize soup (*atole*) and for adults beer, tequila and cigarettes. The altars are lit by candles and perfumed with traditional copal incense. The dead are expected to return to share once again in the sensual joys of life on earth. At the family burial plot, relatives gather to hold celebrations including dancing, singing and feasting at the graves of their departed. These festivities are complemented by an open-air Roman Catholic mass.

FLOWERS BLOOM

Each year the people of Tenochtitlán held the festival of Tlaxochimaco ('Coming Forth of Flowers') in honour of ancestors and, in particular, in celebration of the lives of those who had died in the last year. In the first days of the festival, the people gathered wild flowers in the fields near the city and carried them to the temple as an offering to the ancestral tribal god Huitzilopochtli and to Tezcatlipoca, one of the gods of death. They performed ritual dances in memory of the deceased.

The Maya, by contrast, were profoundly fearful of death despite the fact that it was as frequent a visitor among them as it was among the Aztecs. Far from celebrating those who had departed the earth, the bereaved made great demonstrations of their grief with wails of despair by night and floods of tears by day.

Funerary customs also varied among the cultures of Mesoamerica. The ancient way, which was followed widely in the

Above: These figures are part of a procession of gods and goddesses painted on the walls of a noble burial chamber (Tomb 105) in Monte Albán, probably in c.AD500–750.

Below: A skull decorated with shell and jade was laid in the tomb of an Aztec noble who went fearlessly to the spirit world.

settlements of Oaxaca, in Teotihuacán, in Veracruz and throughout Maya regions, was to bury the body in a shroud with a funerary mask for the wealthy and a range of offerings connected to the person's livelihood when alive. The Toltecs and their followers in the Postclassic Period, including the Aztecs, preferred cremation. The body was wrapped in bandages and tied in an upright, seated position before being burned; the resulting ashes were then buried with funerary offerings. Some members of the Aztec elite, however, were granted burial.

RICH AND POOR BURIALS

The burials of rulers, nobles and the wealthy were considerably richer than those of commoners. Elite graves in Classic-Period Maya cities were rich in offerings of jade and serpentine, in funerary masks, jewels and splendid clothes.

In some special cases a pyramid-temple might be erected or an existing structure refashioned to encompass a tomb for the deceased king. A high-ranking scribe would be buried with the pens and other equipment he used to ply his elite trade.

Commoners were generally buried beneath the floor of their houses. In time, as relatives died and were buried

alongside them, the house would be abandoned and used as a family shrine. According to Bishop Diego de Landa, a commoner in Yucatán would be buried in his cotton robe with a few grains of maize or jade beads in his mouth. These would sustain or support him on his voyage along the white road of the Milky Way to the underworld.

Above: Zapotec nobles were buried. Urns such as this one, found in Tomb 113 in Monte Albán, were not used to contain ashes and must have had a ceremonial use.

SACRIFICED IN DEATH

From the 10th century on, the Mixtecs broke open the graves of Monte Albán's former Zapotec rulers and used them to bury their own elite. They left magnificent grave offerings in gold and silver. Slaves and dogs were killed and interred to mark the rank of their former master.

Sacrificial burial appears to have been a Mesoamerican practice as far back as the time of Teotihuacán. A series of burials beneath the Pyramid of the Feathered Serpent contain 137 bodies with hands tied behind the back. Scholars believe they were killed as an offering to the gods upon the completion of the pyramid *c.*200AD.

Left: The snake, a complex symbol of new life and of the earth, is depicted consuming a human skeleton in a carving from Tula.

INDEX

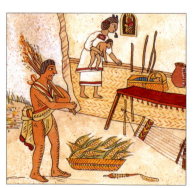